CHICKEN WAS ONCE AN EXPENSIVE
LUXURY – TO BE SERVED ON SUNDAYS
OR ON SPECIAL OCCASIONS. TODAY IT IS
CHEAP, EASILY AVAILABLE AND PART
OF MOST FAMILIES' STAPLE DIET.

And chicken doesn't have to be roasted on Sunday, curried on Monday ... You can bake it with pineapple; cook it with brandy and peaches; casserole it in cider; glaze it with orange; serve it in a traditional Kentish Pie or Provencal Casserole.

Try a Walnut and Chicken Loaf, Sweet and Sour Chicken, Cheese and Chicken Soup, Paté or even Drunken Chicken.
You will find all these delicious recipes and many more, from Britain and around the world, in 'THE CHICKEN COOKBOOK'.

Also by ANNE MASON

AUSTRALIAN COOKING
SWISS COOKING
COOK FOR TOMORROW
FREEZE FOR TOMORROW
STARTERS AND AFTERS

The Chicken Cookbook

Anne Mason

CORGI BOOKS
A DIVISION OF TRANSWORLD PUBLISHERS LTD

THE CHICKEN COOKBOOK
A CORGI BOOK 0 552 98099 4

First publication in Great Britain

PRINTING HISTORY
Corgi edition published 1980

Copyright © Anne Mason 1980

Conditions of sale

1. This book is sold subject to the condition that it shall not, by way of trade *or otherwise*, be lent, re-sold, hired out or otherwise *circulated* without the publisher's prior consent in any form of binding or cover other than that in which it is published *and without a similar condition* including this condition being imposed on the subsequent purchaser.
2. This book is sold subject to the Standard Conditions of Sale of Net Books and may not be re-sold in the U.K. below the net price fixed by the publishers for the book.

This book is set in Linotype Times 10/11

Corgi Books are published by Transworld Publishers Ltd., Century House, 61–63 Uxbridge Road, Ealing, London, W5 5SA

Made and printed in Great Britain by
Richard Clay (The Chaucer Press) Ltd, Bungay, Suffolk

Contents

Introduction	2
Weights, Measures and Temperatures	4
American Cooking Terms	5
Kitchen Equipment	6
Facts About Chicken	9
Freezing Chickens	10
French Cooking Terms	11
To Cook Giblets	12
Herbs for Flavour	14
Soups	17
Main Dishes with Whole Birds	29
Main Dishes with Chicken Pieces	58
Salads, Cold Dishes and Patés	101
With Chicken Livers	124
With Chicken Breasts	135
Sauces and Stuffings	144
Cooking on Skewers	157
With Leftovers	162
Chicken for Slimmers	172
Acknowledgements	177
Index	179

Introduction

Introduction

Chicken was once an expensive luxury meat, served only on Sunday or special occasions. Today, thanks to the growth and efficiency of the chicken farming industry and the availability of both whole birds and chicken pieces at a wide range of prices, chicken is within the reach of every purse. Suitable for family meals any day of the week, it can be used in a wide variety of dishes.

Chicken is international, and there are few countries which do not include some chicken dishes in their national cuisine, while it is a symbol of hospitality in many Eastern countries.

I have tasted chicken cooked in champagne and curacao in Barcelona; enjoyed chickens cooked in coconut shells in Samoa; in hollowed-out fresh pineapples in Hawaii, and with cherries in Russia. Chicken basted with honey and mustard was served to me in Copenhagen, and honey and mixed spices were used to baste the chicken I ate at an Arabian dinner. I have a recipe from a Chinese friend—but have never tried it—for cooking a whole chicken inside a watermelon, and the best chicken salad I ever tasted was served in halved avocados at Surfer's Paradise in north-eastern Australia.

It has been interesting to collect recipes from those places I have visited, but it has also been rewarding to investigate some of the old country dishes from British farm kitchens, such as Kentish Chicken Pudding and Kentish Pie from the pleasant county where I now live; or the Cock-a-Leekie of Scotland and the Ffowlyn Cymreig or chicken casserole with cabbage of Wales, all of which you will find in this book.

And among these recipes you will find suggestions to suit every taste and for every occasion all through the year, from family meals to formal dinner parties, for even with the enormous numbers of chickens sold every day—there is still something special about a chicken dinner.

Weights, Measures and Temperatures

Weights, Measures and Temperatures

Although metrication is already in our kitchens by way of cans and packages it will probably be some time before today's housewives discard their old kitchen scales and favourite measuring cups and spoons.

But metrication has been included in schools for some time, and the coming generation of cooks are already counting in metric. Unfortunately, there has been much controversy about what amounts should be used, but the Metrication Board and the United Kingdom Federation for Education in Home Economics have recommended that metric recipes should be based on a weight unit of 25 grams representing one ounce, and one pint is represented by 500 millilitres (half a litre).

There is no simple relationship between metric and imperial quantities, and exact conversion of recipe quantities is not practicable. To achieve good results there has to be some adjustment and the two sets of ingredients are not interchangeable. The recipes in this book are written to give successful results whether you use metric quantities or the old imperial quantities, but you must keep to one method or the other. The new metric amounts give a slightly smaller amount than the imperial measures in the finished recipe.

For the benefit of those who prefer to keep on using their familiar spoons and cups for measuring the following table will be useful:

> 15 ml spoon equals approximately 1 tablespoon
> 10 ml spoon   "   "   1 dessertspoon
> 5 ml spoon   "   "   1 teaspoon
> 2·5 ml spoon   "   "   ½ teaspoon

These metric spoons come in sets of four. Metric measuring jugs are also available, the most practical metric marking is in steps of 50 ml.

Where cups have been used in recipes here I have used a standard 10 ounce measuring cup, which in metric terms would be a 250 ml cup, or measure.

If making American recipes it should be noted that the US cups contain only 8 ounces, whereas ours are 10 ounce, and the US pint is 16 fl oz against the Imperial pint of 20 fl oz or 500 ml. At the time of writing, USA has not gone over to the metric system of measurements, but it is expected that this will take place in the future.

In Australia the measure of 30 g to the ounce has been adopted, with 1 lb replaced by 500 g, and 1 tablespoon is 20 ml, while 8 fl oz (1 cup) is 250 ml.

When buying new scales it is important to see that they are calibrated in steps of 5, 10, 20, 25 and 50 g up to at least 1 kilogram.

Existing baking tins and kitchenware can still be used, but if buying new ones look for those marked in metric measurements.

Oven Temperatures: In metric the measurement of temperature is the degree Celsius (formerly called centigrade), which is written °C. Temperature markings on electric cookers are now in C; the numbers on gas cookers remains the same. The following table shows the metric against the old measures.

Heat of oven	Deg F	Deg C	Gas Mark
	225	110	1/4
Very slow	250	130	1/2
	275	140	1
Slow	300	150	2
	325	160	3
Moderate	350	180	4
	375	190	5
Moderately hot	400	200	6
	425	220	7
Hot	450	230	8
Very Hot	475	240	9

This is an approximate guide only, as different makes of cookers can vary. If in any doubt refer to the manufacturer's chart which comes with your cooker. The heat referred to is in the centre of the oven.

Always pre-heat your oven to the required temperature before putting in the food to be cooked. It is a good idea to have your automatic heat control checked by a qualified mechanic at regular intervals.

American Cooking Terms

For those who like to use American recipe books it is well to know the differences in the cooking terms used by British and American cooks, some of which are given here.

British	USA
plain flour	all-purpose flour
cornflour	cornstarch
fat such as butter, margarine or white vegetable fat	shortening
icing sugar	confectioner's sugar
icing (for cakes)	frosting
treacle	substitute molasses
wholemeal flour	substitute Graham flour
wholemeal or digestive biscuits	substitute Graham crackers
plain dry biscuits	crackers
sweet biscuits	cookies
scones	biscuits
jelly (as in packaged, flavoured gelatine)	Jello
jam	jelly
sultanas	seedless raisins
melted butter	drawn butter
bicarbonate of soda	baking soda
frying pan	skillet
pastry tarts or flans	pies
pies	deep-dish pies
broil	grill

Kitchen Equipment

No matter what kind of a kitchen you have in which to prepare your meals you can still have the help of proper equipment for cooking. Having the right tools for the job can make a great deal of difference to the amount of time and work you put into your cooking.

A cook is a craftsman just as much as a carpenter or a plumber and you would not expect them to do a good job unless they had the proper tools. It is the same with cooking. So whether you are starting from scratch, or buying new kitchenware to replace those which have worn out, try and buy the best you can afford, and choose it carefully to suit your needs.

If your family enjoy casserole cooking, buy several sizes in ovenproof glass or pottery and one fairly large size in flameproof cast-iron and enamel, such as the French Le Creuset ware, which can be used on top of the stove or in the oven and looks nice to bring to the table to serve. One large enough to take a whole chicken is very useful.

Invest in a good thick baking dish for roasting, and a thick frying pan—one with a lid is most useful. When buying new saucepans look for a flat base, straight sides and an insulated handle, and a close-fitting lid. If you cook on an electric or solid-fuel stove such as an Aga you need heavy gauge aluminium or stainless steel saucepans with thick, flat bases. All these may be more expensive to buy but they give you better service for many years cooking. And don't forget a non-stick milk saucepan.

Good sharp kitchen knives in various sizes are essential; a pair of sharp scissors and a pair of poultry shears are two items I could not work without, also a small potato and vegetable peeler. Wooden spoons, flexible spatulas and a special egg-slice to go with the non-stick finish of your frying pan, these are extras you can buy one at a time, also a good stiff vegetable brush.

Except for my electric kettle, the most used piece of electrical equipment in my kitchen is my blender (liquidiser) which whips, grinds, shreds and purées various foods to whatever consistency you wish.

A pressure cooker is invaluable for making stock and cooking all those foods which need long, slow boiling.

But we all have our own individual needs, depending on the type of cooking we like to do, and every kitchen is a workshop fitted out to suit the person working in it. One important thing to remember is that every piece of equipment in your kitchen should work for you, and if it doesn't do that get rid of it and don't have it cluttering up your cupboards.

Facts About Chicken

Facts About Chicken

Today's oven-ready chickens are young birds of between 2½ and 4 lb (approximately 1·1 and 2 kg), with a bland delicate flavour quite unlike that of an older free-range bird, and they need care in cooking to enhance this blandness. There is a tendency among cooks accustomed to free-range birds to overcook today's frozen chickens, which should be cooked more slowly—simmered not boiled—and the heat lower than usual for grilling and roasting.

Chicken is a lean meat, particularly high in protein and with a good nutritional value. The fat and cholesterol content is low, making it an excellent meat for those on a fat-free or reducing diet (see p. 172). Readily digested, particularly the breast meat, it is ideal for children and invalids as well as for the heartiest and hungriest appetites.

New techniques in farming mean that chicken is obtainable in shops all through the year with consistent quality. With its bland flavour it mixes well with many different textures and flavours, such as the tang of lemon, the crunch of nuts, the richness of cream, the aroma and flavour of fresh herbs and with different wines, while a plain boiled chicken can be 'dressed up' for a special occasion with a tasty sauce (see p. 144).

A whole bird is best value for money when catering for the average family. Choose a bird by weight, allowing about ½ lb (200 g) uncooked chicken per portion. The bones and giblets can be used for making stock or soup.

A whole bird will take longer to cook than pieces, and care should be taken to avoid overcooking by checking the weight of the bird. Calculate the roasting time after thawing and after the giblets have been removed from inside the bird. Allow 20 minutes per pound, plus 15 minutes, cooking in a moderate oven (350°F, 180°C or No. 4), testing the leg with a skewer for tenderness when you consider it has cooked long enough. Cooking in foil takes a little longer.

Chicken pieces are good buys for quickly cooked meals, or for casseroles, and when only one or two serves are needed. They are excellent for fried or grilled chicken and for many other recipes given here.

When buying frozen birds be sure their wrappings are intact and there are no freezer burns on the skin. Be sure to thaw completely before cooking, whether using a whole bird or pieces. A whole bird should be placed in the refrigerator or a cool larder for 24 hours to thaw, pieces should thaw in 4 to 5 hours at room temperature.

If you are in a hurry to cook a frozen chicken, leave in its wrapping and immerse in *cold* water until it has thawed through. Never pour boiling water over an unwrapped bird or you will take away its taste. Be sure to remove the packet of giblets inside bird before cooking.

When thawed, do not keep a whole chicken more than 12 hours before cooking, and cook chicken pieces within 8 hours of thawing. Keep in refrigerator or cool larder until ready to cook, and any leftover cooked chicken should be returned to the refrigerator as soon as it is cold, covered with foil or film to keep it moist. Do not keep for more than two days.

Tasty ways of using leftover chicken can be found on page 162.

A chicken dinner can be a contradiction, because an old bird can taste as good as a spring chicken if it is carefully cooked. Whether you use a free-range fowl from your own farmyard, a boiling fowl from the butcher or one from the deep-freeze, the result depends on the cooking.

Freezing Chickens

Unless you raise chickens in your own backyard or have a friend who keeps free-range birds, it is hardly worthwhile for the housewife to freeze chickens at home. But if you are lucky enough to keep a flock of birds, and have somebody to kill and pluck them for you, here are a few tips.

When choosing young birds to freeze see that the breast bones are soft and flexible; they should be plump and covered with flesh, and firm to the touch.

The birds should be cleaned, plucked and trussed before freezing, the giblets should be cleaned and either wrapped in foil or in a small polythene bag and frozen with the chicken, but not inside it—the bird will thaw quicker if frozen empty. If a bird is stuffed before freezing this shortens its freezer life, so it is best to do this when ready to cook.

Freshly killed poultry will keep in the freezer for 9 to 12 months, but if filled with stuffing should only be kept for three months. Older birds should be cut into joints ready for casseroles or longer cooking.

The bones of all poultry are apt to turn dark after more than three months in the freezer, but this in no way affects the flavour or nutritional value of the bird.

When storing frozen birds from the supermarket they should be left in their original wrapping, then placed in a freezer bag, labelled with date of purchase and weight. Unless there is a date stamp on the store label it is uncertain how long they have been frozen, so it is wise to use up supermarket birds within two months of purchase.

Cooked foods have a shorter storage life than when frozen uncooked so it is advisable to use up cooked dishes within two months of freezing. There is no health hazard from keeping longer, but the quality, flavour and appearance will gradually deteriorate the longer they are kept in the freezer.

French Cooking Terms

For those who like to follow French recipes the following terms may be helpful.

Very young baby chickens (sometimes called squab) chickens are known in culinary French as *poussins*. They range from 1 lb (400 g) to 1¾ lb (700 g) oven-dressed.

Spring chickens, aged from 4 to 8 months and weighing not more than 2½ lb (1·1 kg) are called *poulets de grain* or *poulets reine*. In America they are referred to as *broilers*.

Boiling hens, rather aged but still with good flavour and plenty of meat, are known as *poules*.

The *suprêmes* are the correct name for the meat on each side of the breast from the point when the wing starts to the extremity of the stomach. They are also known as *filets de volaille*, and are traditionally the choicest cuts of the bird. Care should be taken not to overcook these, and they can be gently poached or rolled in seasoned flour and very quickly fried until golden on both sides (see p. 135).

Capons are de-sexed young male birds weighing not less than 4 lb (2 kg) and usually not more than 8 lb (4 kg), with tender flesh and good flavour.

On a French menu a poulet sauté means a chicken cut into joints, fried gently in butter or oil, then either stock or wine is added, with perhaps vegetables or bacon. If tomatoes are added it will be called Provençale; if with mushrooms it will be either Chasseur or Forestière; a Poulet Sauté Célestine will have tomatoes, mushrooms, wine and cream, and is named after one of the Emperor Louis Napoleon's chefs. If it is garnished with asparagus tips it will be named Poincaré, after a famous French politician, and Parmentier means it has cubes of potatoes in it, named after Antoine Augustin Parmentier who introduced potatoes into France in the 18th century, and also invented twenty different ways of cooking them.

Poulet Sauté Dauphinois is chicken cooked with whole garlic cloves, preferably garlic from Provence, and was supposed to be a favourite with a Dauphine of France. Many other chicken dishes are known by the name of the town or province where they originated, or the chef who first made them.

To Cook Giblets

When buying oven-ready frozen chickens, inside each one you will find a polythene-wrapped parcel of giblets. These should always be removed from the bird before cooking. They can be cooked with the bird for extra flavour, made into giblet gravy or cooked with the carcase for making stock.

The giblets should consist of the heart, liver, gizzard and neck, and if buying fresh undressed birds be sure and ask the poulterer for the giblets and feet after he has cleaned the bird for you. The feet can be scalded and skinned (cut off toe-tips) and added to giblets for extra strength. Wash giblets well and remove skin from gizzard before cooking.

The liver can be put aside and used in the stuffing or the gravy, but if cooking with the giblets it should be added for the last 15 minutes cooking time only, as long cooking makes it tough. Recipes for cooking chicken livers can be found on pages 124.

To make stock, cover giblets with cold water, adding salt, a bay leaf and a sprig of thyme or parsley and simmer gently for 30 to 40 minutes. Strain and use either for making gravy or a sauce for the chicken.

The weights given here are for dressed birds, including the giblets. It should also be remembered when buying frozen birds that there is a slight weight loss when bird is de-frosted.

The number of serves given for the following recipes are only an approximate guide to help the cook, and are very flexible. Appetites vary and serves may need to be either larger or smaller to suit individual tastes.

Herbs For Flavour

Herbs for flavour

The clever cook soon learns how valuable herbs can be for flavouring various foods, and chicken benefits greatly by the addition of certain herbs in a number of dishes. We all know of sage and onion or parsley and thyme for stuffing, and all through this book there are recipes using various herbs, both fresh and dried.

Herbs are very easy to grow, and even those people without a garden can grow the most useful ones in pots on a sunny window ledge or in a window box. In the garden the best place to grow your herbs is in a small patch close to your back door so that they are easy to get to when you need to pick them fresh. Choose a sunny, well-drained spot where the soil is not too rich, give them room to grow and don't water them too much. Parsley and chives are an exception to this, they need good soil and plenty of water, but I have fresh parsley all through the winter growing in a large pot on my kitchen window-sill.

Dry your herbs for use in the winter. They are best gathered when quite dry, preferably in the morning after the dew has dried out but before the sun gets too hot. Spread them out in a single layer on paper on a flat tray and place in an airing cupboard or *above* the oven when it is in use. Dry the herbs until they are brittle but still rather green in colour, and when quite dry rub them to separate leaves from the stems. Sieve if necessary. Store in airtight jars away from light and heat, labelled with name and date. Use them up—don't forget about them, for they lose their flavour if stale.

The most useful herbs are parsley, chives, garlic, thyme (in various flavours), sage, mint, tarragon and basil, and if you like experimenting try dill and chervil. Most good nurseries can help you with either established plants or with seeds, or if you have a friend with a herb garden you could ask for roots of both thyme and mint which always grow prolifically and need regular thinning out. Bay leaves are also most useful but these are bought already dried in packets.

When the term 'bouquet garni' is used in a recipe it means a bouquet of fresh herbs tied together to facilitate its removal before serving the dish. It usually consists of a bay leaf, sprigs of fresh thyme, parsley and perhaps tarragon or marjoram or rosemary.

The flavour of dried herbs is much more concentrated than when fresh, so halve the quantities of dried herbs used if directions are given for fresh herbs in a recipe.

For those who are just beginning to use herbs it is best to start experimenting with very small amounts in a dish carefully following tested recipes in which herbs are used. This is the best way to find out what herbs are best for your own taste or that of your family, but care must be taken that the herb or herbs used do not predominate to such an extent that the main flavour of the dish is lost.

Parsley is probably the most useful of all herbs, used both in cooked dishes and as a garnish. Don't throw away the stems, which can be chopped with the leaves to give extra flavour. I never chop parsley, but use a pair of sharp kitchen scissors to snip the tightly-bunched parsley heads and then the stems; this saves the loss of juices which take place when parsley is chopped on a board. Scissors should also be used for chives.

Use the young green leaves of celery as well as the stalks; the green stems of spring onions or shallots; crush a clove of garlic by placing it beneath the flat of a knife and then giving it a hard knock—peeling it first, of course.

If you haven't already got one, invest in a pepper grinder, for freshly ground pepper has much more pungency than the kind you buy as a fine powder. Both black and white pepper come from the same peppercorns, only the black contains the outer skin and has more taste. Use white pepper for sauces or delicate foods as the flecks of ground black pepper would spoil the appearance.

Soups

Soups

Chicken stock can be the basis for a number of appetising soups, and stock can be obtained either from the liquor in which you have boiled a fowl or from the carcase after you have removed the meat for a meal.

Never throw away the skin and bones without getting the last scrap of value from them, but when using the carcase do not include any of the stuffing as it clouds the stock. If the giblets have not been used to make stock for the gravy, they should be added to the carcase to provide extra strength to the stock.

When home-made stock is not available chicken stock cubes can be used, but be careful not to overseason, as the cubes are already salted.

Basic Chicken Stock

1 chicken carcase
1 onion, quartered
2 carrots, chopped
1 stalk celery
sprigs of parsley
sprigs of thyme
1 bay leaf
4½ pints (2·5 litres) water

Break the carcase into pieces and put into large saucepan with any skin, giblets, prepared vegetables and herbs. Add cold water and bring slowly to the boil. Simmer until reduced by about one-third, about 1½ hours, then strain into a bowl and leave to cool. Store in refrigerator and use within three days. Skim off fat before using.

If you have a pressure cooker use only half the amount of water and cook under pressure for 15 minutes, then allow pressure to reduce gradually. As in this way you get a more concentrated stock, water can be added to make up the required quantity.

Creamy Chicken Soup

2 pints (1 litre) stock
4 oz (100 g) cooked chicken
1 oz (25 g) butter *or* margarine
1 oz (25 g) flour
4 tbsp top milk *or* cream
salt, pepper and nutmeg

Put chicken meat and 1 tbsp stock through electric blender. Melt butter, stir in flour and cook for 2 minutes, then slowly stir in stock until it boils and thickens. Stir in puréed chicken, add top milk or cream and season to taste, re-heat but do not allow to boil. Sprinkle each serve with parsley. Serves 4.

Chicken and Vegetable Soup

Follow previous recipe but add 1 or 2 diced, cooked carrots to chicken when putting through blender. In place of parsley as a garnish add 2 tbsp cooked peas.

Giblet Soup—Pressure Cooked

Chicken giblets can usually be bought in any good poultry shop and they make a good, nourishing soup.

2 tbsp butter or margarine	1 rasher bacon, chopped
1 lb (400 g) chicken giblets	2 or 3 sprigs parsley
2 tbsp flour	1 bay leaf
2 medium onions, sliced or 3 sticks of celery, diced	salt and pepper
	2 pints water

Melt butter in pressure cooker. Wash giblets well and roll in flour, then fry in the hot butter for 2 or 3 minutes, turning to fry evenly. Add onion and fry for a few minutes. Add the remainder of ingredients, fix lid and bring to 15 lb pressure, cooking under pressure for 15 minutes. Reduce pressure under cold water, remove lid and strain soup. Taste for seasoning, and add a little milk if necessary, re-heating but do not boil. Serves 5 or 6.

German Giblet Soup

Use the giblets of a large boiling fowl for this soup, and if you have the feet of the bird the soup is even better.

giblets and legs of a large bird	1 lb (400 g) potatoes
1 large onion, sliced	salt and pepper
2 leeks, chopped	1 tbsp chopped parsley
2 carrots, sliced	2 tbsp sour cream

Wash giblets well, cut neck into several pieces, discard skin and claws from feet and put all into a large saucepan of cold water. Bring to boil and add prepared vegetables, except potatoes, and simmer for 1½ hours, covered. Strain stock, remove legs, and put aside the vegetables and giblets. Cook the peeled, sliced potatoes in the stock until very soft. Put potatoes and vegetables through a sieve or electric blender with a little of the stock. Chop heart and gizzard very small, strip meat from neck (be careful of small bones), and add with puréed vegetables to stock with parsley. Re-heat and serve at once, adding a small spoonful of sour cream to each soup bowl. Yogurt may be substituted for the sour cream if preferred. Serves 4–5.

Chicken Petite Marmite

Deliciously warming for a cold day and substantial enough to be served as a first course for lunch.

1 cup cooked, shredded chicken	2 pints (1 litre) chicken stock
½ cup cooked, diced carrots	6 rounds buttered toast
½ cup cooked peas	grated Parmesan cheese
½ cup cooked, sliced celery	

Combine chicken, vegetables and stock and bring to boiling point. Divide between 6 ovenproof soup bowls and flat a piece of buttered toast on top of each bowl, sprinkle with grated cheese and put into hot oven just long enough to lightly brown the cheese.

If more convenient, the buttered toast can be sprinkled with cheese, put under a griller and browned lightly, then floated on top of the soup. Serve at once. Serves 6.

Crème St Germain

A delicately flavoured soup to make with fresh spring peas.

1 pint (500 ml) chicken stock	¼ pint (150 ml) water
1½ lb (700 g) young green peas	2 tbsp butter *or* margarine
1 leek, including green part	pinch salt and sugar
3 young lettuce leaves	3 tbsp thin cream

Shell peas, wash leek well and slice thinly, shred lettuce. Melt butter in saucepan and cook vegetables for 3 or 4 minutes, add water and seasoning, cover and cook until vegetables are tender. Remove 2 tbsp peas for garnishing, and put remainder of vegetables through sieve or electric blender. Add stock and bring to boil, then add cream and re-heat if necessary, but do not allow to boil. Place a few peas in each soup bowl and serve soup at once. Serves 4.

Rice Soup with Chicken Livers

2 pints (1 litre) chicken stock
2 oz (50 g) long-grain rice
2 oz (50 g) chicken livers
1 oz (25 g) butter
chopped parsley *or* chives
salt and pepper

Bring stock to boil and add rice, boil for 15 minutes until soft. Meanwhile, fry chopped chicken livers in butter for only a few minutes and add to soup with parsley or chives. Season to taste and serve at once. Serves 4.

Consommé Avocado

A delicious soup for a dinner party, yet simple to prepare.

2 large, ripe avocados
2 pints (1 litre) clear chicken stock
½ cup dry white wine
2 tbsp grated Parmesan cheese
salt and pepper to taste

Be sure the avocados are ripe enough to be tender when pressed gently between the palms. Peel very thinly as the pale green colouring is just below the skin and this gives the soup an attractive colour. Cut pulp into thin, neat slivers, cover with wine and soak for an hour or two. When ready to serve bring stock to the boil, add wine drained from avocados and re-heat. Divide avocado pieces between six soup bowls and pour soup over them, then sprinkle with cheese and serve. Serves 6.

Summer Day Avocado Soup

Ideal for a summer's day luncheon is this cold soup from the Bahamas. Lime juice is called for in the original recipe but if unobtainable, lemon juice may be used.

4 cups cold chicken stock
2 cups peeled and chopped avocado
salt and pepper to taste
6 tsp sour cream *or* yogurt
2 tbsp lime or lemon juice

Put chopped avocado through electric blender or press through a sieve with a little of the stock. Add to remainder of stock with lemon juice, season to taste. Chill until ready to serve, divide between 6 soup bowls and garnish each with a spoonful of yogurt or sour cream. Serves 6.

Egg Drop Soup

This is a typical Chinese soup, simple to make and attractive to serve for dinner.

2½ pints (1·4 litres) chicken stock
3 eggs
2 tsp soya sauce
1 spring onion, chopped

Heat chicken stock in saucepan. Beat eggs well with wire whisk and pour in a slow, thin stream into the boiling soup, whisking continuously. Reduce heat, add soya sauce and simmer for about 1 minute. Serve at once, garnishing each bowl with a little of the finely chopped onion.

This is also a good soup for an invalid, omitting the soya sauce and using parsley instead of onion. Serves 6.

Chicken, Egg and Lemon Soup

This is a classic Greek soup, enjoyed by plutocrat and peasant alike.

2 pints (1 litre) chicken stock
2 oz (50 g) rice
2 eggs
juice of a large lemon
salt and pepper

Bring stock to the boil in a large saucepan, and while boiling quickly throw in rice. Boil 15 minutes until rice is tender. Whisk eggs with lemon juice, then add 3 or 4 tbsp of hot stock to egg mixture, whisking continually. Remove stock from heat, pour in the egg mixture, whisking all the time, and serve at once. Do not re-heat once eggs have been added or the mixture will curdle. Serves 4–5.

Cream of Celery Soup

1 head young celery
1 large onion
1 large potato
1 tbsp butter *or* margarine
2 pints (1 litre) chicken stock
½ pint (250 ml) milk
salt and pepper
grated cheese

Wash and cut up celery, including freshest and youngest leaves. Peel and slice onion, peel and cube potato. Heat butter in a large saucepan and cook celery and onion until golden, add potato and stock and bring to boil, then simmer gently for 20 minutes until vegetables are tender. Rub through a sieve or put through an electric blender.

Return to saucepan with the milk, season to taste and re-heat. Serve sprinkled with grated cheese. Serves 6.

Bacon and Corn Chowder

6 rashers streaky bacon, diced
½ cup chopped onion
1½ pints (850 ml) chicken stock
1 lb (400 g) can cream-style corn
salt and pepper
1½ pints (850 ml) milk
½ cup thick cream
1 tbsp chopped parsley

Fry bacon until crisp in a large saucepan. Put half the bacon aside. Add onion to bacon fat and sauté until soft. Add chicken stock and bring to the boil, then add corn and milk and simmer for 15 minutes. Remove from heat, add cream, reserved bacon, parsley, and taste for seasoning. Serve at once. Serves 6.

Potage Paysanne

A hearty soup for a cold day.

2 pints (1 litre) chicken stock
1 leek, chopped
1 carrot, chopped
1 turnip, chopped
1 large potato, peeled, diced
4 oz (100 g) peas
4 young cabbage leaves
½ cup parsley
few sprigs fresh thyme
1 tbsp lemon juice
salt and pepper
½ pint (250 ml) milk
1 cup diced chicken meat
sour cream

Put prepared vegetables into a large saucepan with the stock, parsley and thyme and simmer all together until soft. Put all through a sieve or electric blender. Add milk, lemon juice, salt and pepper to taste and the diced chicken meat and re-heat. Serves with spoonfuls of sour cream on top of each serve. Serves 6.

Majorcan Chicken Soup

This is almost a meal in itself when served with crusty garlic bread.

4 oz (100 g) streaky bacon, diced	½ sweet red pepper, sliced
1 tbsp oil	bay leaf
1 large Spanish onion, chopped	2 pints (1 litre) chicken stock
1 lb (400 g) chicken meat, diced	1 lb (400 g) cooked potatoes
1 lb tomatoes, peeled, chopped	salt and pepper
	chopped parsley

Heat oil in large saucepan and fry the bacon until crisp. Remove from pan and fry onion until transparent, then add chicken and cook for 5 minutes, turning frequently. Add pepper (be sure all seeds are removed), tomatoes, bay leaf and chicken stock and simmer, covered for 30 minutes. Add diced potatoes and bacon pieces and cook for another 5 minutes. Taste for seasoning and divide between six soup bowls, add parsley to each bowl and serve at once.

If a thick, smooth soup is preferred cook soup for 10 minutes longer and put through a sieve or electric blender. If a blender is used it will be necessary to strain the soup to remove the tomato seeds. Alternatively, use 2 tbsp tomato paste instead of fresh tomatoes, and garnish soup with the crisp bacon dice. Serves 6.

Potage Crecy

This is a soup which can be served either hot or cold, depending on the weather.

2 oz (50 g) butter *or* margarine	chopped parsley or chives
1 onion, chopped	2½ pints (1·4 litres) chicken stock
1 lb (400 g) carrots	salt and pepper
½ lb (200 g) potatoes	½ tsp sugar

Peel and grate carrots on coarse grater, peel and dice the potatoes. Heat butter in large saucepan and fry onion until transparent but not browned. Add carrots and potatoes and turn in the butter for 2 or 3 minutes, then add stock and seasonings and simmer, covered, for about 30 minutes. Rub through a sieve or put through an electric blender.

If serving hot, re-heat and serve sprinkled with parsley or

chives. If serving cold, chill and turn into 6 soup bowls, add a spoonful of fresh or sour cream to each one and sprinkle with chives. Serves 6.

Creole Soup

1 large onion, chopped	2 pints (1 litre) chicken stock
1 oz (25 g) butter *or* bacon fat	1 lb (400 g) tomatoes
½ green pepper, seeded	1 small can sweet corn
½ sweet red pepper, seeded	chopped parsley
1 tbsp cornflour	

Peel tomatoes and remove seeds, or use canned tomatoes and put through a sieve.

Brown onion in fat until golden, then add chopped peppers and cook for 2 minutes. Blend in cornflour and cook for a few minutes, then slowly add stock, stirring until mixture boils. Add prepared tomatoes, cover saucepan and simmer for 20 minutes, add sweet corn, season to taste and bring back to boiling. Serve sprinkled with parsley.

If any leftover chicken meat is available it can be diced and added to the soup with the sweet corn. Serves 6.

Zuppa Pavese

A well-known Italian soup which makes a good snack for lunch.

2 pints (1 litre) chicken stock	4 small eggs
4 thick slices French bread	parsley sprigs
olive oil	grated Parmesan cheese

Fry bread in oil on both sides, then drain well on kitchen paper. Place a slice in each soup bowl. Heat stock to boiling. Carefully break an egg on to each slice of bread and gradually pour the hot stock over each egg to poach it slightly. Add parsley and sprinkle with Parmesan cheese.

If preferred, the eggs can be lightly poached before adding to the bread slices, then the stock is poured around and not over the eggs. Serves 4.

Minestra di Fagioli

Another Italian soup from the province of Tuscany, the English translation being haricot bean soup.

6 oz (150 g) haricot beans
1 clove garlic, chopped
1 medium onion, chopped
1 medium carrot, chopped
salt and pepper
2 tbsp olive oil
2½ pints (1·4 litres) chicken stock
2 tbsp chopped parsley

Soak haricot beans overnight. Heat oil in a large saucepan and cook onion and garlic for a few minutes, then add drained beans, vegetables and half the stock. Bring to the boil and simmer, covered, until beans are tender, about 2½ hours.

Rub soup through a sieve or put through an electric blender, return to saucepan and add remainder of the chicken stock, the parsley and heat slowly. Taste for seasoning and serve. Serves 4 or 5.

Russian Rice and Lemon Soup

3½ pints (2 litres) chicken stock
4 tbsp cooked rice
1 sliced lemon
juice ½ lemon
1 tbsp chopped dill *or* parsley

Bring seasoned stock to boil and add rice and lemon juice and simmer for several minutes. Drop in lemon slices and continue simmering for 5 minutes. Serve in six soup bowls and sprinkle with dill, or if not available, with parsley. Serves 6.

Chicken Liver and Noodle Soup

2 pints (1 litre) chicken stock
3 oz (75 g) fine noodles
8 oz (200 g) cooked peas
salt and pepper
8 oz (200 g) chicken livers
1½ tbsp butter
grated Parmesan cheese

Bring stock to the boil and add noodles, cooking for 10 minutes or until tender. While noodles are cooking fry the sliced chicken livers in the butter, turning at intervals. Add peas, chicken livers and the buttery pan juices to the stock and noodles, re-heat and serve sprinkled with cheese. Serves 4.

Potage DuBarry

1 large cauliflower	salt and pepper
2 stalks celery, chopped	dash cayenne
1 medium onion, chopped	1 tsp curry powder
4 tbsp chopped carrot	½ pint (250 ml) milk
3 tbsp butter *or* margarine	2 tsp lemon juice
2 pints (1 litre) chicken stock	chopped parsley
1 clove garlic, crushed	2 tbsp flour

Wash cauliflower well and divide into pieces, put aside ½ cup tiny flowerets for garnishing. Heat butter in large saucepan and sauté the cauliflower and other vegetables until well softened. Stir in flour and cook for several minutes, then stir in stock, bring to the boil stirring all the time. Add seasonings, cover and simmer for 30 minutes, until cauliflower is tender. Put through a sieve or electric blender, add milk and re-heat, then add lemon juice and taste for seasoning.

Divide the reserved cauliflower flowerets between six soup bowls and pour soup over the top, sprinkle with finely chopped parsley and serve at once. Serves 6.

Pumpkin Soup

Instead of cauliflower use 1½ lb (700 g) peeled, cubed pumpkin when making above recipe, which gives a pleasant orange coloured soup, which is enhanced by using orange juice instead of lemon, and floating a slice of orange in each soup bowl to serve. Serves 6.

Chicken Hurry-Curry Soup

Canned soups can be very useful in an emergency, and with a little imagination can be made more interesting.

2 cans condensed cream of chicken soup	3 tbsp grated apple
milk *or* chicken stock	1 tbsp mango chutney, chopped
½ to 1 tsp curry powder	dash of cayenne

Make up soup with milk or chicken stock as directed on label. Mix curry powder with a little water and stir into soup with grated apple and chutney, mix well and bring to boil. Float a half slice of lemon on each serve. Serves 6 or 7.

Chicken in the Corn Chowder

Almost a meal in itself, this would be good for supper on a cold winter's night.

2 cans condensed cream of chicken soup
milk *or* chicken stock
1 medium can cream-style sweet corn
1 tbsp chopped parsley
dash of paprika

Make up soup as directed on label with milk or chicken stock. Add sweet corn and parsley and bring to boil, serve in six soup bowls and sprinkle with paprika. Serves 6 or 7.

Chicken and Cheese Soup

1 can condensed cream of chicken soup
1 can milk
4 oz (100 g) cottage cheese
1 tsp Worcestershire sauce
chopped chives

Combine all together and serve chilled. Serves 4.

Main Dishes with Whole Birds

Main Dishes with Whole Birds

After completely thawing out the chicken (page 9) and removing the bag of giblets, make sure the inside of the bird is clean. Some people consider that washing out the bird is unnecessary and destroys the flavour, but I like to rinse it out with *cold* water before cooking. It can then be stuffed at the neck end and the skin folded over and secured with small poultry skewers or sewn with needle and coarse thread to keep the stuffing in place. Do not fill bird too full as the stuffing usually swells with cooking. A variety of tasty and unusual stuffings can be found on page 151.

For the sake of appearance and easier carving the bird should be trussed before cooking. Lie bird on its back, fold wing tips back towards the backbone and press legs into sides. If you have a trussing needle thread it with clean, fine string and pass the needle through the first wing joint, through the bird and out through the wing joint on the other side. Tie the ends with a bow for easy removal after cooking. Make a slit in the vent and put the tail (the 'parson's nose') through this. The legs may be tied firmly together through the parson's nose.

Don't forget to remove string before carving and serving.

Roast Chicken

This method of cooking is suitable only for younger free-range birds, and the average size frozen chickens. Prepare the bird and stuff it, place in a roasting tin with melted fat, lay a rasher of fat bacon over the breast and roast for desired time (20 minutes per pound, plus 15 minutes, in moderate oven), basting occasionally. If browning too quickly cover breast with foil or buttered paper. Potatoes may be roasted around the bird at the same time.

An older bird should be steamed or boiled first for 45 to 60 minutes if it is desired to serve it as roast chicken. It is best to cook it the previous day so that it is cold before the stuffing is added. Then roast for 45 to 60 minutes, or until tender when leg is tested with a skewer.

Steamed or Boiled Chicken

1 boiling fowl
1 small onion
few slices lemon

sprigs fresh thyme and parsley
1 bay leaf
salt

Wash the bird, put peeled onion, herbs and lemon slices inside it and tie neatly in shape with fine string. Rub all over with a cut lemon, place on a rack in a deep saucepan and add enough boiling water to come half-way up the bird without covering the breast. Simmer gently for 1 to 2 hours, depending on age and size of bird, but do not overcook or it will fall to pieces. Test leg with skewer to see when it is tender.

Remove from saucepan and cool, removing lemon and herbs from inside. If the bird is to be served cold, some people prefer to allow it to cool in the stock in the saucepan.

If serving hot, make Béchamel sauce (page 144) with half milk and half the strained stock after skimming off the fat, and add chopped capers or parsley, diced asparagus or chopped ham and serve over the sliced meat which can be re-heated in a casserole if necessary.

The well-washed giblets can be put into the saucepan with the bird (not left inside) to make a better stock. After removing bird from saucepan, strain the stock and leave to get cold, then skim off the fat. Store in refrigerator, or this stock can be frozen to be used later for sauces or soups.

Spit-Roasted Chicken

Many cookers have a spit-roast attachment which is ideal for cooking chickens. The bird should be washed inside then trussed firmly and the spit rod inserted through the bird from the neck to just above the tail. Most spits have special fork tines so that the bird can be made really secure. Rub bird over with butter or oil, sprinkle with salt and pepper and cook for $1\frac{1}{4}$ to $1\frac{1}{2}$ hours, depending on size.

While cooking, the chicken should be basted frequently with butter or oil, or melted bacon fat can be used, which gives the skin a well-flavoured crispness. When cooked the drumsticks will be tender when tested with a skewer and will move easily.

Somerset Chicken

Farmers' wives in Somerset make delicious cottage cheese and they find more uses for this cheese than I had ever imagined, including this way of cooking chicken with a cottage cheese stuffing.

3 lb (1·3 kg) chicken
2 small onions, chopped

salt and pepper
chicken liver, chopped

2 tsp mixed herbs
1 cup day-old breadcrumbs
flour
2 oz (50 g) butter, melted

If frozen chicken is used, thaw completely and remove giblets. Wipe inside and outside the bird in cloth wrung out in warm, salted water.

Mix together cottage cheese, onions, herbs, chicken liver, breadcrumbs, salt and pepper, blending well together, and place inside bird. Truss securely with thin string or fasten with poultry skewers. Dust bird all over with seasoned flour, place in baking dish and pour melted butter over. Cover with buttered paper or foil and roast in moderate oven (375°F, 195°C or No. 5) for 1 to 1¼ hours until tender, basting occasionally. Remove paper or foil for last 20 minutes cooking time to brown evenly. Make gravy by thickening juices in pan with a little flour. Serves 5–6.

Hungarian Chicken Smitane

Sour cream is a feature of many Hungarian dishes, and here it blends well with roast chicken.

3 lb (1·3 kg) chicken
1 large onion, finely chopped
2 tbsp butter
½ cup dry white wine
½ pint (250 ml) sour cream
juice ½ lemon
3 cups hot cooked rice
salt, pepper and paprika

Prepare chicken for roasting, rub all over with butter and place in moderate oven (350°F, 180°C or No. 4), cooking for 1 to 1¼ hours until tender, basting at intervals. When cooked, remove bird from pan and keep hot while you make the sauce.

In the fat in the roasting pan cook onion until soft but not browned, add wine and blend with juices in pan, add lemon juice and sour cream, heating together without allowing to boil.

Place chicken on serving dish, arrange rice around it and pour the sauce over the top. Sprinkle with paprika for colour. Serves 5–6.

Chicken and Onion Bake

3 lb (1·3 kg) chicken
pinch mixed dried herbs
1 beef stock cube
6 medium onions, sliced
1 oz (25 g) butter *or* margarine
1 tbsp plain flour
3 rashers streaky bacon
salt and pepper

Remove giblets from chicken, wash well and place in saucepan with herbs and enough water to cover. Bring to boil, cover and simmer for 30 minutes. Strain stock from giblets into a measure, dissolve stock cube in hot giblet stock, then make up to ½ pint (250 ml) if necessary with water.

Peel onions and slice fairly thickly, fry in butter or margarine for about 5 minutes until golden, but not browned. Stir in flour and cook for 1 minute, then stir in stock and bring to boil, stirring continuously until it thickens. Taste for seasoning.

Have the chicken prepared for roasting and place in roasting dish, preferably an ovenproof dish which can be brought to the table for serving. Pour the onion sauce around the chicken. Remove rind from bacon and arrange over the breast of chicken. Cook in a moderate oven (350°F, 180°C or No. 4) for 1 to 1¼ hours, or until chicken is tender, removing bacon for last 15 minutes cooking time for breast to lightly brown. Crumble the bacon into pieces and add to sauce.

Cook potatoes in their jackets in the oven at the same time and serve a green vegetable with the chicken for colour. Serves 4–5.

Orange Glazed Chicken

Prepare chicken for roasting, filling with orange and herbs stuffing (page 152). Brush over with melted butter. Half an hour before end of calculated cooking time brush chicken over with a syrup made of 3 tbsp orange juice and 3 tbsp clear honey. Baste at intervals.

When chicken is cooked, remove from pan, keep hot and make gravy from pan drippings. Serves 4–5.

Roast Chicken with Pineapple

This combination of chicken and pineapple is a very popular one in many countries, and I have tasted variations on this theme in Australia, South Africa, Hawaii and California, and this dish is most attractive to serve for a dinner party.

3½ to 4 lb (1·5 to 1·8 kg) chicken	2 tbsp melted butter
salt and pepper	1 medium can pineapple slices
	walnut halves

For the stuffing:

1½ oz (40 g) butter
1 cup day-old breadcrumbs
4 oz (100 g) pineapple slices
2 oz (50 g) walnuts, chopped

1 tsp grated lemon rind
salt
pineapple juice

Remove giblets from chicken and wash well. Sprinkle inside of bird with salt and pepper and stuff with following mixture.

Melt butter in a small pan, add breadcrumbs and stir and cook for a minute, then add drained chopped pineapple and remainder of stuffing ingredients, adding just enough pineapple juice to give a moist consistency. Pack this loosely into neck cavity and truss bird. Place chicken in roasting pan on a trivet or rack, brush with melted butter and cover with buttered paper. Add giblets (except liver) in pan and add 2 tbsp pineapple juice to pan. Cook in a fairly moderate oven (375°F, 190°C or No. 5), basting bird at intervals. Remove paper about 20 minutes before completion of cooking, and add liver to pan.

Brush pineapple rings over with butter and heat in oven. When bird is cooked, place on heated serving dish and arrange pineapple rings topped with walnut halves around the dish. Keep hot while you make gravy.

Add ½ pint (250 ml) water to giblets in roasting pan, boil fast for 5 minutes and scrape up the residue in the pan, then strain. Taste for seasoning and serve separately in a gravy boat.

If preferred, the gravy can be thickened with a little flour before straining. Peas are the best vegetable to serve with this, or you may prefer just a mixed salad. Serves 5-6.

Mexicana Chicken

The variety of flavours blend well together in this dish from Mexico. Serve it garnished with small bunches of seedless grapes, and accompanied by a dish of cooked rice to which toasted, shredded almonds have been added.

3½ lb (1·5 kg) chicken
½ cup chopped onion
½ cup chopped, seeded green pepper
2 tsp chopped parsley
1 chopped clove of garlic

2 tbsp butter
salt, pepper and dash cayenne
1 tsp ground ginger
1 cup dry white wine
8 oz (225 g) canned tomatoes
2 rashers streaky bacon

Remove giblets from chicken, wash them carefully and put aside the liver. Cover with cold water in a saucepan, bring to the boil, then simmer while chicken is roasting. This gives you stock for the gravy.

Clean chicken inside and out and dry. Mix together the onion, garlic, green pepper, parsley, salt, pepper, pinch cayenne, ginger and 1 tbsp melted butter and place inside bird. Truss securely. Rub bird over with remaining butter and place in baking pan, arrange bacon rashers over breast. Bake in a moderate oven (350°F, 180°C or No. 4), pour wine over the bird and baste at intervals. After 45 minutes, add chopped tomatoes and their juices to the pan and the chopped chicken liver, mixing in with the drippings. Remove bacon rashers, chop them into small pieces and add to pan, then continue cooking until bird is golden brown and tender.

Remove bird and keep hot. Skim off excess fat from pan, then add enough strained giblet stock to make a thin sauce, stirring well as the mixture boils. The gravy may be thickened with a little flour if desired, but it is best left fairly thin to serve over the rice.

Serve the chicken on a heated dish, surrounded with rice and almonds and pour the sauce over. Garnish with the green grapes, or if not available, stuffed green olives may be used as a garnish. Serves 4–5.

Cypriot Rice-Stuffed Chicken

The cooking of Cyprus is a mixture of Greek and Turkish dishes, and this is a typical Cypriot way of cooking a chicken.

3½ to 4 lb (1·5 to 1·8 kg) chicken	1 tsp salt
1½ cups rice	½ cup sultanas
3 cups chicken stock *or* water	1 tbsp sugar
3 oz (75 g) butter or margarine	1 tsp ground cinnamon
3 tbsp blanched almonds, chopped	extra melted butter

Prepare chicken ready for stuffing. Do not wash rice but rub it clean with a cloth. Heat butter or margarine in fairly large thick pan and fry rice until transparent, turning frequently. Add almonds and fry until golden, then stir in water or stock and boil rice until cooked but still firm. Add well-washed sultanas (or seeded raisins), sugar, cinnamon and salt to taste.

Stuff chicken with this mixture, fasten securely and place in roasting pan. Brush over with melted butter and roast in moderate oven (350°F, 180°C or No. 4) until tender, basting at intervals. A piece of foil or buttered paper can cover the breast for the first half of roasting time, then removed to brown bird evenly. If liked, 2 tbsp Cypriot white wine can be added to the pan and used for basting. Serves 5–6.

Poussin Arabian

Something exotic from Arabia such as a wife might serve to her husband as she tell him Tales from the Arabian Nights.

2 lb (900 g) chicken	sugar
2 tbsp honey	preserved ginger
2 oz (50 g) butter	fresh *or* canned cherries
1 tbsp blanched, chopped almonds	watercress

Melt butter and warm honey, then mix together. Prepare bird for roasting, and prick all over the breast with a sharp-pointed knife. Brush over with the honey-butter mixture, and pour the remaining honey inside the bird. Place in baking pan and roast in moderate oven (350°F, 180°C, No. 4) for about 45 minutes, or until quite tender, basting at intervals.

When cooked, remove from pan and cut bird in halves through the breastbone, replace in pan breast-side upwards, sprinkle with almonds mixed with a little sugar and replace in oven just until sugar has melted and slightly caramelised. Place chicken on heated serving dish and garnish with sliced ginger, cherries and watercress. Just before serving spoon over juices from baking pan. Serve with rice. Serves 2.

Tandoori Chicken

If you have tasted Tandoori Chicken in Indian restaurants you might like to try this rather Anglicised version which is hot and spicy just as served in Tandoori restaurants, but cooked in a modern oven instead of the specially built clay ovens which use the fiercer heat of charcoal. The chicken must be prepared at least eight hours before it is to be cooked, so make allowances for this timing when planning this recipe for dinner.

It should be accompanied to the table by little dishes of finely chopped onion, lemon quarters dipped in chopped parsley, shredded lettuce and fried puppadums.

2½ to 3 lb (1·1 to 1·3 kg) chicken
salt and pepper
3 cloves of garlic
1 inch (2·5 cm) stem ginger
1 tsp chilli powder
1 tsp cummin
1 tsp mixed spice
½ tsp turmeric
1 tsp chopped mint
¾ pint (400 ml) yogurt
butter

Clean and remove skin from chicken (use with giblets to make stock), make small cuts in legs and breast and rub all over with salt and pepper, leave for 1 hour.

An Indian cook would use a mortar and pestle for the next stage, but you could use an electric blender if you prefer. Grind into a paste the garlic, ginger, spices and yogurt and rub this mixture well into the chicken all over, then leave to soak up the mixture for at least six hours.

When ready to cook wrap the chicken in buttered foil, sealing the foil parcel very firmly. Bake for an hour in a moderate oven (350°F, 180°C, or No. 4), open up the foil and baste the bird with the remaining yogurt mixture, then return to oven until nicely browned.

Cut into four pieces to serve, accompanied by coconut rice. This is made with coconut milk obtained by soaking 8 tbsp desiccated coconut in 2 pints (1 litre) water, then bringing it to the boil, and standing for 15 minutes. Drain off the liquid, pressing with the back of a spoon to obtain the last drop.

Fry 2 tbsp chopped onion in butter in a large pan, add 1 lb (400 g) Patna rice and turn in the butter with a fork, then add coconut milk and salt and cook rice until tender, adding more boiling water if necessary as the rice cooks. Serves 4.

Portuguese Pink Chicken

In Portugal they call this 'Galinha Corda', but Pink Chicken is easier to remember. I tasted it first at the State-run pousada or inn at Obidos, a perfect example of an old walled town, where the food served includes many tasty examples of traditional Portuguese country cooking, accompanied by the good local wines.

4 lb (1·8 kg) chicken	4 oz (100 g) butter
2 tsp salt	4 rashers lean bacon
1 tbsp paprika	½ cup Madeira wine

Cream the butter with the salt and paprika and rub the bird all over with this mixture. Any left over should be placed inside the bird, which should be trussed securely. Place in baking dish and cover breast with bacon slices. Bake in a moderate oven (350°F, 180°C or No. 4) for 1 hour, basting with half the wine, then remove bacon and continue cooking for another 25 to 30 minutes, adding remainder of wine, until bird is tender.

Cut in pieces to serve, with the pan-gravy poured over the pieces. Serves 6

Welsh Chicken

Welsh housewives know this dish as 'Ffowlyn Cymreig' and it is a good way of cooking a rather older boiling fowl.

1 bird	1 oz (25 g) flour
½ lb (200 g) bacon	¾ pint (400 ml) chicken stock
2 large leeks	1 small cabbage, chopped
½ lb (200 g) carrots	bunch mixed herbs
butter	salt and pepper

Clean and truss bird as for boiling. Cut bacon, leeks and carrots into dice. Using a saucepan large enough to take the bird, melt some butter and fry the diced vegetables for a few minutes, then stir in flour and half the stock, stirring until thickened. Place the chicken in the sauce, add the cabbage, herbs, salt and pepper and remainder of stock, bring to boil then allow to simmer for 1½ to 2 hours, until bird is tender.

To serve, make a bed of cabbage on a heated serving dish and place bird on it, then pour sauce from the pan over the top. Serves 6.

Chicken and Leek Pie

This is another recipe from Wales, and I was told this pie is a great favourite to serve on St David's Day, March 1, to honour the country's patron saint. As the national emblem of Wales, leeks are a very popular vegetable in the principality.

3½ to 4 lb (1·5 to 1·8 kg) chicken
1 onion, halved
1 bay leaf
salt and pepper
parsley stalks

2 *or* 3 leeks
8 oz (200 g) short pastry
1 egg
¼ pint (150 ml) cream
chopped parsley

Prepare chicken by trussing and place in large saucepan with onion, bay leaf, salt and parsley stalks and just cover with cold water. Bring to boil, then simmer, covered, for 45 minutes. Remove pan from heat and allow chicken to cool in the liquid.

When quite cold lift fat from surface of stock and remove bird. Cut meat from the bones (remove skin or not as desired) and cut flesh into bite-size pieces. Measure ½ pint (250 ml) stock, putting aside remainder for stock or soup. Trim leeks, leaving some of the tender green parts, slit in halves lengthwise and wash well, then chop coarsely.

Place a layer of chicken in a buttered 2½ pint (1·4 litres) pie dish, cover with a layer of leeks and continue with these layers until ingredients are used up. Season with salt and pepper, and then add the measured chicken stock.

Roll out pastry large enough to cover pie dish, allowing a strip of pastry for around the rim, dampen edges before covering with pastry lid, then trim and seal edges together. Make a few slits for steam to escape and trim with pastry leaves. Brush top of pie over with lightly beaten egg mixed with a tbsp of water.

Bake pie in centre of moderately hot oven (375°F, 190°C or No. 5) for 25 minutes, then reduce heat to 325°F, 170°C or No. 3 and bake for a further 15 minutes until pastry is cooked through and golden on top. When ready to serve cut out a small portion of the pastry and pour in the warmed cream, replace pastry and serve sprinkled with finely chopped parsley. Buttered carrots would be a good vegetable to serve with this. Serves 6.

Curried Chicken with Spaghetti

This is a splendid way of cooking an old bird and making it give enough to serve 10 or 12 people for a buffet party when you need at least one hot dish. It can be prepared ahead of time and just re-heated in a casserole at the last minute.

5 lb (2·3 kg) bird
16 oz (400 g) spaghetti
2 cups chopped green pepper

1 whole onion, halved
1 bay leaf
salt and pepper

2 cups chopped onion
2 cups chopped celery
2 tbsp butter
8 oz (200 g) mushrooms, sliced

14 oz (397 g) can tomatoes
2 tsp curry powder (*or* to taste)
2 tsp cornflour
1½ cups grated cheese

Prepare bird, remove giblets and truss firmly. Wash giblets well and put into large saucepan (except liver) with onion, bay leaf and chicken and just cover with water. Bring to boil then simmer, covered, until tender. Leave in the stock until nearly cold, then remove and strain stock, removing fat from top. Cut chicken into bite-size pieces off the bones.

Sauté the chopped onion, green pepper (be sure and remove the seeds) and celery in butter for 5 minutes, then add mushrooms and chopped chicken liver and cook gently until liver is cooked through, about 6 minutes. The vegetables should still be crisp. Blend in curry powder.

Cook spaghetti in boiling salted water for 10 minutes, then drain well. Mix chicken pieces, spaghetti, vegetables, chicken liver and juices from the pan, then chop tomatoes and add with the juice, putting all into a greased ovenproof casserole.

Thicken ½ pint (250 ml) chicken stock with the cornflour, taste for seasoning and pour over the chicken mixture. Re-heat in moderate oven. The mixture should be thick when served but not dry. Sprinkle with grated cheese before serving.

If casserole is to be prepared ahead of serving time, add the thickened chicken stock just before re-heating.

If preferred, the chicken mixture can be made up as directed then poured over the cooked spaghetti as a sauce, rather than heated all together in the casserole. In this case more chicken stock should be added as the sauce needs to be rather less thick. Serves 10–12.

Cock-A-Leekie

This is a very famous traditional Scots dish, which is both a stew and a soup. It properly calls for an old cock past its prime, but today's boiling fowl is more usual for the modern housewife.

4 to 4½ lb (1·8 to 2 kg) bird
1 large veal *or* beef marrow bone
3 rashers bacon, chopped
salt and pepper

12 leeks
1 cup cooked prunes
1 bay leaf
sprigs fresh thyme and parsley

Prepare the bird, trussing it firmly. Wash the leeks well, and using only the white part, slice thinly. Put into large saucepan with the bird, bacon, marrow bone and herbs, cover with water and bring to boil. Simmer, covered for 2 to 2½ hours or until bird is tender.

Traditionally, the bird should then have all the meat taken from the bones in pieces and added to the strained stock with the stoned prunes, and eaten as a soup-stew in bowls. But modern taste usually prefers the bird to be removed from the stock and served as a main course with a sauce made by pressing the leeks and the marrow from the bone through a sieve, adding just enough stock to make a good consistency. Reheat this sauce with the prunes and serve with the bird.

The remainder of the stock can be served as soup, garnished with a few pieces of chicken sliced thin and some chopped parsley. Serves 6.

Cheshire Chicken

A very simple way of cooking a chicken in a fairly large metal casserole. This comes from Cheshire.

Add the chopped chicken liver to an ordinary breadcrumb and herb stuffing and stuff the prepared bird. Melt about 4 oz (100 g) butter in a metal casserole and turn the bird in the hot butter until it is a good golden colour all over.

Place lid on casserole and put into a moderate oven (350°F, 180°C or No. 4) and let the chicken cook in the butter until nearly tender, breast side downwards. Half-way through cooking time turn bird over, baste well and season with salt and pepper, then continue cooking until completely tender, removing lid for last ten minutes. Serve sprinkled with finely chopped parsley. Serves 4–5.

Lemon Chicken

Lemon trees grow in nearly every garden in Greece, and lemons are used in many Greek dishes, such as this way of cooking an older bird.

4 to 4½ lb (1·8 to 2 kg) chicken
1½ lemons
8 oz (200 g) onions, sliced
8 oz (200 g) carrots, chopped

2 oz (50 g) butter *or* margarine
4 oz (100 g) blanched almonds
¼ pint (150 ml) white wine
1 egg

3 stalks celery, chopped
8 oz (200 g) mushrooms, sliced
few sprigs fresh thyme and parsley
½ pint (250 ml) chicken stock
4 tbsp cream
salt and pepper

Remove giblets and clean bird. Squeeze juice from the whole lemon and paint bird with the juice. Sprinkle with salt and pepper and leave for 15 minutes. Place the half lemon inside bird and truss firmly. Place in a deep saucepan with onion, carrot, celery and herbs, just cover with water and bring to boil. Simmer gently for 2 to 2½ hours, until tender, time depends on age of bird. Remove and keep warm, covered with buttered paper. Remove lemon from inside bird.

Strain the stock. Cook mushrooms in butter for 8 to 10 minutes, add ½ pint (250 ml) stock, wine and almonds and heat without boiling. Beat egg and cream together and pour hot mixture over them, stirring all the time, until mixture thickens.

Serve chicken on a bed of rice, pouring the mushroom mixture over the top. Serves 5 or 6.

Cretan Chicken

The market in Heraklion in Crete is, like most Mediterranean markets, a very colourful sight with its great variety of vegetables. It also has the best herb stalls I have seen anywhere. This is a variation on the above recipe as I tasted it in this very pleasant island.

Cook bird as in previous recipe until tender, then remove and keep warm. Strain the stock, pressing vegetables through a sieve.

Chop 1½ lb (700 g) peeled, ripe tomatoes and 1 red and 1 green pepper (remove seeds) and cook in a little butter or oil until tender. Stir in just enough stock with the sieved vegetables to make a good sauce, season to taste and bring to the boil.

Serve chicken on a bed of rice and pour the tomato sauce over the top.

Chicken Normandy

Calvados is a type of spirit distilled from cider in Normandy and is used in many dishes by the local housewives. A similar spirit is known in America as applejack. If neither is available cider can be used, but the flavour will not be as strong.

4 lb (1·8 kg) chicken
salt and pepper
2 oz (50 g) butter
1 large onion, chopped
1 lb (400 g) eating apples
2 fl oz (50 ml) Calvados
½ pint (250 ml) chicken stock
finely grated rind ½ lemon
½ tsp dried sage *or* 2 fresh sage leaves

Rub the chicken over with salt and pepper after removing giblets. Using a large flameproof casserole, melt butter, add chicken and cook, turning frequently, until it is golden brown all over. Remove from casserole and keep warm.

Add onion to butter in casserole and cook for 6 to 7 minutes until soft but not browned, then add the peeled, cored and quartered apples and continue cooking for 2 minutes, turning to cook evenly. Add stock, Calvados, sage and lemon rind and bring to boil, stirring. Return chicken to casserole, and baste well with the liquid, cover and place in a moderate oven (350°F, 180°C or No. 4) for about 1 hour or until tender.

Remove casserole from oven and carefully lift chicken on to a heated serving dish. Using a slotted spoon, lift out the apple quarters and arrange around chicken. Skim as much fat as possible from the surface of the sauce in the casserole, pour half the sauce over the chicken, and serve remainder separately in a gravy boat. If preferred, the sauce can be thickened with a little cornflour but do not make it thick and gluey. Remove sage leaves if used.

Another version of this recipe omits the apples from the casserole in the beginning, and instead the apples are not peeled but cut into rounds, the cores removed, and the apples poached in the juices in the casserole after bird is removed. This helps to keep their shape when used as a garnish. Serves 4–5.

Brandied Chicken with Peaches
Follow above recipe, omitting the apples and sage and replacing the Calvados with brandy. When chicken is cooked, remove from casserole and keep warm, then poach canned peach halves in the juices in casserole. Serve chicken, garnished with the peach halves and the gravy from the casserole.

Poule au Pot
There are many versions of this Chicken in the Pot, a well known French dish which tradition says that good King Henry

of Navarre wished in the early 17th century that all his people might be prosperous enough to eat it on every Sunday of the year. It is certainly an excellent way of cooking a good fat boiling fowl, and you need a large deep saucepan so there is plenty of room for the bird and the vegetables.

4 lb (1·8 kg) boiling fowl	salt and pepper
chicken liver	butter *or* bacon fat
4 oz (100 g) pork sausage meat	½ lb (200 g) bacon *or* gammon in one piece
2 tbsp soft breadcrumbs	
milk	turnips, carrots, onion, celery, leek
1 large egg	
1 tbsp chopped parsley	1 bay leaf

Remove giblets and wash well, and clean bird inside and out. Make the stuffing with the chopped chicken liver, sausage meat, breadcrumbs soaked in milk and squeezed dry, parsley, salt and pepper and lightly beaten egg. Fill bird with this mixture and truss well.

Melt butter or bacon fat in the large saucepan and brown bird all over. Add giblets, chopped vegetables, salt, pepper and bay leaf and enough boiling water to cover the bird. Bring to the boil and skim off any scum on top, cover pan and simmer slowly for 2 to 2½ hours, or until bird is tender. Carefully remove bird from saucepan and keep hot while you make the sauce.

Remove giblets, bacon piece and bay leaf from stock and strain into a basin, skimming fat from top. (Keep this fat for cooking another chicken). Press the vegetables through a sieve and add just enough stock to make a thin sauce. Add chopped bacon and re-heat, then pour over bird. Serves 6.

Poule en Daube

This is the previous recipe served cold instead of hot. In place of the bacon add a small veal bone when cooking bird. When quite tender remove bird from stock, strain stock and put back into saucepan with the veal bone to continue boiling for a further 30 minutes to reduce. Skim off any fat.

Carve the bird as you would for serving, but re-assemble the pieces into its former shape on a serving dish. Pour the strained stock over the bird and leave overnight to set.

Capon à la Basque

The Basques are a somewhat mysterious people, living on the border of Spain and France, yet not belonging to either country and with their own language and customs. But their cooking resembles that of Spain more than France, and this is a typical recipe for cooking a large fat capon, or you could use a large boiling fowl, which would take a little longer to cook. You need a large deep saucepan for this.

1 capon *or* boiling fowl	1 large clove garlic
8 oz (200 g) garlic sausage, in one piece	2 inch strip orange peel
	1½ lb (700 g) ripe tomatoes
8 oz (200 g) streaky bacon, in one piece	2 red peppers
	1 green pepper
1 carrot, sliced	¾ lb (300 g) rice
1 onion, sliced	1 tsp paprika
1 bay leaf	1 tbsp butter
oil *or* lard	chicken giblets
salt and pepper	

Heat oil or fat in saucepan and brown bird on all sides, remove from pan and fry onion and carrot for a few minutes, turning frequently. Replace bird and add bacon piece, bay leaf, peeled and crushed garlic and strip of orange peel. Add enough boiling water to cover bird, bring to boil then allow to simmer gently until tender, about 2 hours or depending on age of bird. Add garlic sausage 20 minutes before cooking time is completed.

Remove bird when cooked, cut in serving pieces and keep hot. Remove bacon and garlic sausage and keep hot. Strain stock and remove as much fat as possible from top.

While chicken is cooking, cook rice in boiling, salted water for 12 to 15 minutes until tender, drain well and rinse under hot water. Cover with a clean cloth and keep hot in colander over boiling water.

Make sauce by cooking the peeled, chopped tomatoes and seeded, sliced peppers in butter for 10 minutes, turning frequently. Season with salt, pepper and paprika and add just enough chicken stock to make a good sauce.

Arrange rice as a border on a large serving dish, cut bacon in cubes, peel and slice sausage and arrange with chicken pieces in dish. Pour sauce over the top and serve at once. Serves 6–7.

New England Boiled Chicken Dinner

Good, plain cooking is a tradition in New England states of America, and this is a favourite dinner.

4 lb (1·8 kg) boiling fowl	1 small cauliflower
salt and pepper	6 carrots
1 bay leaf	1 tbsp chopped parsley
3 large potatoes, peeled and halved	2 tbsp flour
	¼ cup thick cream
6 small onions	chicken liver
3 stalks celery, sliced	

Prepare fowl for boiling, removing giblets, and trussing bird firmly. Place in large saucepan with bay leaf, salt and pepper and cover with boiling water. Bring to boil and simmer, covered, until bird is nearly tender, about 1½ hours.

Cut carrots in halves, lengthwise; break cauliflower into florets and add with remainder of vegetables, also the chopped chicken liver, to the chicken. Continue cooking until bird is quite tender and vegetables are cooked.

Lift fowl on to heated serving dish and surround with the well-drained vegetables. Strain some of the stock and thicken with flour, then stir in cream, stirring over low heat until thickened. Serve gravy separately. Serves 6.

Market Day Chicken

An ideal way to cook an old bird when you will be out shopping all day, and can leave this to cook very slowly in the oven, as farmers' wives used to do on market day.

1 plump old hen	4 sliced onions
1 cup rice	2 stalks celery, with leaves
2 pints (1 litre) milk	freshly grated nutmeg
salt and pepper	1 bay leaf
few sprigs fresh thyme	chopped parsley

Prepare the bird for cooking and place in a deep ovenproof casserole. Add rice, onion, herbs and seasoning and half the milk and cover tightly. Put into a very slow oven (250°F, 120°C, or No. ½) and leave it to cook, looking at it after a couple of hours to see if it needs more milk, as it probably will. Give it a stir at the same time, then leave it for another hour or so. When absolutely tender, dish it up with the rice all around it, and serve with a green vegetable for colour.

This is also good if you have an electric slow-cooker. Serves 4 or 5.

Chicken with Tarragon

A delicious French dish if you have tarragon growing, or you can use dried tarragon if necessary

3½ lb (1·5 kg) chicken
2 oz (50 g) butter *or* margarine
2 tbsp chopped fresh tarragon
  or 2 tsp crushed dried
  tarragon
1 clove garlic

salt and pepper
½ pint (250 ml) chicken stock
2 tbsp brandy *or* dry sherry
4 tbsp thick cream
1 bay leaf

Clean chicken, removing giblets and washing them well. Put giblets into small saucepan with bay leaf, cover with water and bring to boil, then boil gently for 30 minutes.

Cream together the butter or margarine with the tarragon and peeled and crushed garlic, salt and pepper. Spread tarragon butter over the bird, placing any leftover inside. Stand for 30 minutes for flavours to permeate bird, then place on a rack, lying on its side, in a roasting pan. Strain the stock from the giblets into the pan, and place in fairly hot oven (400°F, 200°C or No. 6) for 20 minutes. Turn chicken on to other side, baste well and roast for another 20 minutes, then turn bird breast upwards, baste and roast for another 20 minutes, or until bird is tender when leg is tested with a skewer.

Remove chicken from pan, place on serving dish and keep hot. Remove rack, pour off as much fat as possible but retaining juices, add brandy or sherry and bring to the boil, then stir in cream. Season to taste and pour into warmed sauceboat.

For those who may not like the distinctive flavour of the tarragon, fresh thyme or parsley may be used instead.

In Denmark, where dill is very popular and fresh dill readily available, chicken is cooked with the dill in the same way as given here for tarragon, and lemon juice is used instead of brandy or sherry. Serves 4 or 5.

Spiced Chicken Pot Roast

Cooked on top of the stove in a large flameproof casserole (I use a Le Creuset which I bought in Paris many years ago and which is ideal for cooking both on top of the stove and in the oven) this is a most useful recipe, as it can simmer away quite happily for extra time if dinner is delayed. And any leftover gravy can be made into a tasty soup for next day.

3½ to 4 lb (1·5 to 1·8 kg) chicken
1 tbsp plain flour
1 tsp salt
½ tsp pepper
½ tsp ground ginger
½ tsp ground cinnamon
½ tsp ground cloves
2 tbsp cooking oil
2 medium onions, chopped
2 large carrots
1 large leek
2 sticks celery
1 tbsp chopped parsley
2 tsp cornflour
½ cup chicken stock
¼ cup white wine
6 button mushrooms, sliced
4 medium tomatoes, peeled

Remove giblets and use to make stock. Wash chicken well, drain and dry. Mix the flour with salt, pepper and spices and rub the chicken all over with this seasoned flour. Heat the oil in the casserole and brown the chicken on all sides, turning frequently to brown evenly.

Slice the carrots and celery, cut leek into short lengths using some of the green part and wash well, then halve lengthwise. Place onion, carrots, leeks, celery and parsley around the bird, add wine and stock and cover tightly. Cook over low heat for 2 hours or longer, depending on size of bird.

About half an hour before bird is completely cooked, remove it from casserole. Mix cornflour with a little water and stir into the casserole, stirring until it boils and thickens, then replace chicken, add mushrooms and sliced tomatoes and continue cooking until chicken is tender. Taste for seasoning.

When ready to serve carve chicken and serve with chopped vegetables from the pot and some of the gravy. Plain boiled potatoes go best with this.

The carcase can be boiled up to make stock and added to the gravy from the casserole to make a good vegetable soup.   Serves 4 to 6.

Virginia Chicken Pie

This is an old country recipe from Virginia, and an excellent way of cooking an older bird.

4 lb (1·8 kg) boiling fowl	1½ cups rice
1 onion, chopped	3 large ears of corn, cooked
1 bay leaf	*or* large can sweet corn
salt and pepper	2 tbsp butter
1 cup chicken stock	1 beaten egg

Prepare fowl and place in a large saucepan with onion, bay leaf, salt and pepper and enough water to just cover bird. Bring to boil then simmer gently until bird is cooked. Cook rice in plenty of boiling, salted water for 12 minutes, drain well and toss with 1 tbsp butter while still hot. Drain fowl and cut meat from the bones in nice even pieces.

Place half the rice in a buttered baking dish which can be brought to the table for serving. Arrange chicken pieces on top, cover with corn scraped from the cobs, or drained canned corn, remainder of rice and pour chicken stock over the top. Dot with remainder of butter, and pour beaten egg over all. Bake in a moderate oven (350°F, 180°C or No. 4) for 30 minutes until golden brown on top. Serves 6.

Honeyed Chicken and Peaches

2½ lb (1·1 kg) chicken	3 oz (75 g) butter
4 fresh peaches	2 tbsp honey
12 cloves	1½ oz (40 g) blanched almonds
½ tsp ground cinnamon	bunch watercress
salt and pepper	

Prepare bird for baking, and put 1 tbsp butter inside it, place in baking tin. Pour boiling water over peaches, leave for 30 seconds then peel off skin. Stick 3 cloves in each peach and place in the tin with the bird. Melt honey, butter and cinnamon together and pour over bird and peaches, cover breast of chicken with foil or buttered paper and roast in moderate oven (350°F, 180°C or No. 4) for 45 minutes, then remove paper and add almonds to the tin. Continue roasting for a further 30 minutes, basting occasionally and turning the almonds. Remove chicken to a hot serving dish, arrange nuts and peaches around it, and garnish with watercress.

The juices in the pan can be thickened to make gravy. Serves 4.

Chinese Glazed Chicken

The glaze gives a piquant flavour to this chicken.

2½ lb (1·1 kg) chicken
1 medium onion, sliced
salt and pepper
1 cup clear honey
1 tbsp soya sauce
2 spring onions, chopped
1 orange, sliced
cucumber

Remove giblets from bird and wash carefully. Place chicken and giblets in a large saucepan with the onion, salt and pepper and just cover with water. Bring to the boil, then simmer gently, covered, for 30 minutes. Allow bird to cool in the stock. When quite cold, drain bird well and cut in halves through the breastbone, lifting out any loose bones. Place cut side down in an ovenproof baking dish.

Mix honey and soya sauce, spread over the chicken and put into a moderate oven (350°F, 180°C or No. 4) for 30 minutes, basting with the honey mixture several times. Serve in the baking dish sprinkled with spring onions and garnished with orange and cucumber slices. Serve boiled rice separately. Serves 4.

Chicken Soubise

Soubise means that a dish is cooked with onions, and this is a simple dish for those who like those fragrant vegetables.

2½ lb (1·1 kg) chicken
1 bay leaf
few sprigs thyme and parsley
salt and pepper
1 lb (400 g) onions, sliced
4 oz (100 g) butter
1½ oz (40 g) flour
¾ pint (400 ml) chicken stock
¼ pint (150 ml) cream
pinch nutmeg
parsley heads for garnishing

Remove giblets and put chicken into a large saucepan with herbs and salt and just enough water to cover. Bring to boil and simmer, covered, for 1¼ hours until tender. Leave in stock while you prepare the sauce.

Melt 3 oz (75 g) butter in a thick saucepan and cook the sliced onions, covered, until tender, but not browned. Stir in flour, cooking for 2 minutes, then stir in hot stock and cook for 15 minutes, stirring occasionally. Put the onion mixture through a blender until smooth, bring again to simmering point and add cream, season to taste and stir in butter until melted, but do not boil. Serve this sauce over chicken, which should be cut into 4 quarters to serve. Garnish with parsley. Serves 4.

Coq au Riesling

I use a Yugoslav Riesling for this recipe, but any fruity white wine is good as long as it is not too sweet. Drink the same wine with the finished dish.

3 lb (1·3 kg) chicken
2 tbsp butter
2 shallots, chopped
½ pint (250 ml) white wine
½ pint (250 ml) chicken stock
2 tbsp chopped parsley
small bunch white seedless grapes
1 tbsp flour
1 egg yolk
¼ pint (150 ml) thin cream
salt and pepper

Melt butter in a large saucepan and brown the chicken on all sides, turning frequently, and keep the pan covered while the bird browns so that it cooks at the same time, but be careful it does not burn. This should take about 25 to 30 minutes. Remove from the pan and cut bird into joints. Add shallots to butter in pan and cook until soft. Replace the chicken in pieces, add wine, stock and parsley. Cover and cook until bird is tender when tested, lift out and keep warm on a serving dish. Scatter the grapes over the top.

Boil liquid in the pan very rapidly to reduce slightly. Skim fat from top. Mix a little stock or water with flour and stir into the hot liquid, stirring until thickened. Mix egg yolk and cream together in a bowl, then strain the liquid in the saucepan over the cream mixture, stirring well. Taste for seasoning, re-heat but do not allow to boil and pour over the chicken. Serve at once. Serves 4 or 5.

Coq au Vin

This is practically a repeat of the previous recipe but instead of Riesling the chicken is cooked in Burgundy or other good red wine.

Fry 4 rashers streaky bacon, chopped, in the saucepan before browning the chicken, then remove while chicken is browning. After chicken has been jointed and replaced in saucepan add the bacon pieces, 12 button mushrooms, a bay leaf, wine, stock and parsley, cover and cook until bird is tender, lift out and keep warm on a serving dish, and surround with the mushrooms.

Thicken the juices in the pan with a little flour, stirring until thick and cook for 2 minutes, then pour over the bird. Don't forget to remove bay leaf before serving. Serves 4 or 5.

Kansas City Chicken

A very imaginative cook who was my hostess in Kansas City gave me this recipe after I had enjoyed the dish at her home, along with a number of other very original dishes. It is her version of the classic boned, stuffed chicken, and can be served either hot or cold.

3½ lb (1·5 kg) chicken
1 lb (400 g) pork sausage meat
12 oz (300 g) can whole kernel corn
butter *or* bacon fat

2 tbsp chopped sweet red pepper
1 tbsp chopped parsley
salt and pepper

Mix together the sausage meat, parsley, sweet corn and red pepper, season with salt and pepper.

Remove giblets from bird and put aside for stock. Wash bird inside and dry carefully. Using a small, sharp knife cut skin on each side of the breast and draw back the skin, being careful it does not tear. Cut down the flesh on either side of the breastbone and fold down the breast and wing meat on either side. With a sharp pair of scissors or poultry shears cut out the breastbone, wishbone and top of the carcase bones as neatly as possible.

Fill the cavity in the bird with the sausage meat mixture, shaping like the original chicken. Fold back the breast meat, draw back the skin and sew back in place with strong thread.

Rub the bird with butter or bacon fat and roast in the centre of a fairly hot oven (400°F, 200°C or No. 6) for about an hour, basting at intervals. Test a leg to see if bird is cooked. If browning too much on top cover with a piece of buttered paper or foil. Potatoes and carrots can be cooked around the bird at the same time if desired.

When bird is cooked, remove from roasting pan and make gravy with the juices in the pan if serving bird hot. Remove threads before carving, cut down the centre of the breast from neck to tail and then cut in thick slices crosswise. Serves 4 to 6.

Mustard Chicken in Foil

A chicken retains all its flavour when cooked in foil, and also saves washing up.

3 lb (1·3 kg) chicken
salt and pepper

2 tsp brown sugar
juice 1 small lemon

1 rasher fatty bacon
sprigs fresh thyme and
  parsley
1 tbsp French mustard

2 oz (50 g) butter
1 small onion, chopped
cooking foil

Prepare the chicken for roasting, placing the fatty bacon and the herbs inside the bird with salt and pepper, and then truss firmly. Mix together softened butter and remainder of ingredients to make a spread, rub well over the chicken on all sides. Wrap in a large piece of cooking foil, sealing the top and ends firmly.

Place wrapped bird in a dry baking tin in a moderate oven (350°F, 180°C or No. 4) for about 1½ hours, or until leg of chicken is tender when tested. Open foil for last part of cooking time to brown on top.

Cook potatoes in their jackets in the oven with the chicken. Serve the juices in the foil as a gravy after skimming off some of the fat, or it can be thickened with a little flour in a small saucepan if preferred. Serves 4 or 5.

Chicken Vieux Carré

The food of New Orleans is a mixture of French and Spanish, known as Creole, and it is usually rich and tasty and always interesting. This is one way of cooking chicken from that lovely city, with its marvellous restaurants and exciting jazz.

3 lb (1·3 kg) chicken
1 pint (500 ml) thick cream
1 tsp made mustard

salt and pepper
1 tsp mushroom ketchup
2 tsp Worcestershire sauce

Roast chicken as directed on page 29. When cooked cut it into serving pieces and arrange in a shallow ovenproof dish. Whip the cream until stiff, then mix in remainder of ingredients and pour over chicken pieces. Return chicken to a moderate oven (350°F, 180°C or No. 4) and continue cooking until topping has browned, but care must be taken that it does not burn.

Cooked chicken pieces can be finished in the same way. Serves 4 or 5.

Austrian Chicken with Noodles

4 lb (1·8 kg) chicken
1 medium onion, sliced

4 egg yolks, well beaten
1 cup hot chicken stock

1 carrot, sliced
1 stalk celery, chopped
salt and pepper
1 bay leaf

1 cup cream
1 lb (400 g) noodles
little butter
grated Parmesan cheese

Clean and truss bird for boiling, adding the giblets to the saucepan with onion, carrot, celery, bay leaf, salt and pepper and enough hot water to barely cover bird. Bring to boil and simmer gently until tender, about 1½ hours. Remove from pan, draining well and cut meat from the bones in neat strips.

Cook noodles in boiling, salted water for 10 or 12 minutes until tender, drain well and put into an ovenproof casserole filling it about half way with the noodles, cover with chicken pieces. Keep hot while you make the sauce.

Put egg yolks into the top of a double boiler over hot water and heat gently. Gradually stir in 1 cup strained chicken stock and the cream, stirring all the time until sauce thickens. Season with salt and pepper and pour sauce over the chicken and noodles in casserole. Sprinkle top thickly with grated cheese and put into a hot oven until golden brown on top. Serve with a green vegetable or a salad. Serves 6.

Mediterranean Chicken

A recipe typical of the cooking of many Mediterranean lands.

3½ lb (1·5 kg) chicken
½ lb (200 g) green bacon, diced
2 tbsp olive oil
2 tbsp butter
½ lb (200 g) button mushrooms

½ lb (200 g) green olives, pitted
1 clove garlic, crushed
salt and pepper
4 to 6 tbsp brandy *or* wine
1 lb (400 g) diced potatoes
4 tomatoes, peeled

Clean and truss chicken. Heat butter and oil in flame-proof casserole and sauté chicken on all sides until golden. Sauté the diced bacon in the casserole, replace chicken and add olives and mushrooms, then pour brandy or wine over bird. Season with salt and pepper, cover and cook over low heat for about 50 minutes. Add potatoes and tomatoes and simmer for another 15 minutes or until chicken is tender. Serve from the casserole. Serves 4 or 5.

Chicken with Rice

This is a simple country dish I have tasted both in France and England—both countries claim it as their own.

4 lb (1·8 kg) chicken	salt and pepper
3 carrots, sliced	1 bay leaf
2 large onions, sliced	½ lb (200 g) rice
6 cups water	chopped parsley

Clean chicken and truss for boiling. Clean giblets and put into large saucepan with the chicken, carrots and onions, bay leaf, salt and pepper and water. Bring to boil and simmer, covered until tender, about 1½ hours. Skim off as much fat as possible, and remove giblets. Bring stock to a gentle boil and add rice, continue cooking for about 20 minutes until rice is quite tender.

Remove chicken and cut into serving pieces, place on a hot serving dish. Strain off any liquid from rice, remove bay leaf, and pile rice around the chicken pieces. Sprinkle with parsley and serve at once.

Brown mushroom sauce (see page 145) could be served with this if you prefer your chicken served with a sauce. Serves 6.

Chicken Waterzoie

This is a famous Flemish dish from Belgium, and like the Cock-a-Leekie of Scotland, is a combination of main dish and soup. It is an excellent way of cooking an older bird.

1 boiling fowl	½ bottle dry white wine
2 onions, stuck with 8 whole cloves	1 halved lemon
	bay leaf
3 stalks celery, chopped	salt and pepper
3 leeks, sliced	chopped parsley
2 carrots, sliced	

Clean and truss fowl. Rub all over with the cut lemon and place in a large saucepan with the prepared vegetables and enough water to cover. Bring to the boil and simmer, covered for 1 hour, then add wine and bay leaf, salt and pepper. Continue simmering until bird is quite tender.

Remove bird from saucepan and cut into serving pieces, then serve in deep soup plates with the stock and vegetables. Discard bay leaf and sprinkle each plate with chopped parsley. Serves 6.

Chicken Navaressa

A recipe for those who have tarragon growing in their garden or can obtain it fresh from a neighbour.

3 lb (1·3 kg) chicken	3 carrots, sliced
4 oz (100 g) ham rasher	2 leeks, sliced
2 tbsp chopped tarragon	bouquet garni
2 oz (50 g) butter	salt and pepper
2 tbsp oil	½ pint (250 ml) white wine
3 onions, chopped	½ pint (250 ml) chicken stock

Mix tarragon, butter, salt and pepper and chill for half an hour. Clean chicken and place tarragon butter inside it, then truss firmly. Place in a large flameproof casserole, brush over with oil and place in a hot oven (425°F, 220°C or No. 7) for 20 minutes to brown. Remove from oven and add diced ham, prepared vegetables, bouquet garni, stock and wine, cover and replace in oven, lowering heat to moderate (375°F, 190°C or No. 5), and cook for about 1 hour, or until bird is tender.

Remove bird from casserole and keep hot. Mix 1 heaped tbsp flour with a little water or stock and stir into the juices in the casserole. Bring to the boil, stirring until thickened. Place chicken on a heated serving dish, surround with the vegetables and ham and pour sauce over the top. Serves 4 or 5.

Russian Chicken with Raisins

3 lb (1·3 kg) chicken	8 oz (200 g) seeded raisins *or*
½ pint (250 ml) milk	sultanas
4 thick slices white bread	salt and pepper
3 tbsp butter or margarine	5 fl oz (150 ml) chicken stock

Cut crusts from bread and soak the bread in milk. Squeeze out the surplus milk. Soak the raisins in hot water for 5 minutes, then drain well and mix with the bread pulp and 1 tbsp melted butter. Clean chicken, removing giblets (use to make the stock), and stuff with the bread mixture. Truss firmly and rub chicken with 1 tbsp of butter. Place in a roasting dish with remainder of butter, cover bird with buttered paper or foil and roast in a moderate oven (350°F, 180°C or No. 4) for an hour or until the bird is tender. Ten minutes before removing bird from oven add chicken stock to the dish and baste chicken, removing the foil or paper to brown on top. Make gravy from pan juices. Serves 4.

Kentish Chicken Pie

An old farmhouse recipe from Kent, using a rather aged boiling fowl.

4 lb (1·8 kg) bird with giblets
6 medium carrots
1 large onion
salt and pepper

short pastry
6 fairly thick slices cooked ham
1 bay leaf
chicken stock

Remove giblets from bird and soak them in cold water for a few minutes. Wash bird and place in a large saucepan with the whole, peeled carrots, sliced onion, bay leaf, salt and pepper and the cleaned giblets, and just cover with water. Bring to the boil and simmer, covered until bird is tender, from $1\frac{1}{2}$ to 2 hours, depending on age of bird.

Remove from pan and cut meat from the bones in fairly large pieces. Slice the carrots and strain the stock from the saucepan. Put alternate layers of chicken, ham and carrots into a deep, buttered pie dish, standing a pie funnel in the centre. When all ingredients have been used up add just enough stock to cover top of filling.

Roll out pastry to fit over pie dish, allowing for a double edge, and cover pie, crimping edges together. Make several slits for steam to escape, brush over with a little milk to glaze and decorate with cut-out pastry leaves. Bake in a hot oven (425°F, 220°C or No. 7) for 35 minutes until golden brown and crisp.

Serve either hot or cold, but if serving cold cut a small hole in the pastry after it is cooked and add as much extra stock as pie will hold. This will jelly and give a good texture when pie is cut cold. Serves 6.

Chicken and Ham Potpie

This is a variation of the above chicken pie, using scone dough instead of pastry as a topping.

Make up the scone mixture with 8 oz (200 g) flour, and add 1 tbsp chopped parsley and $\frac{1}{2}$ tsp dry mustard to the mixture. Roll out to fit over a deep, round ovenproof casserole in which the chicken and ham have been layered as in preceding recipe. Place scone round on top, glaze with a little milk and bake in a hot oven for about 15 minutes until well risen and golden. Serves 6.

Main Dishes with Chicken Pieces

Many dishes call for chicken pieces rather than a whole bird, and convenience packs of frozen chicken joints are ideal for such dishes, or a whole bird can be cut into joints if preferred. Sometimes four joints, such as legs and thighs, are more useful when making a casserole for four people; packs of legs or 'drumsticks' are useful for certain dishes, such as the Honeyed Drumsticks on page 61, and for special occasions the packs of chicken breasts or suprêmes are ideal for such dishes as Suprêmes Garibaldi on page 140.

One advantage of using a whole bird and jointing it is that the trimmings and giblets are available for making stock for sauces and gravies. A pair of poultry shears is useful for jointing the bird.

When no home-made chicken stock is available chicken stock cubes can be used, but be careful of over seasoning as the cubes are usually well seasoned.

One 3½ lb (1·5 kg) chicken after cooking will give about 3 cups of diced chicken meat.

Chicken in Cider

4 chicken pieces
2 medium onions, chopped
3 rashers bacon
1 oz (25 g) butter
1 tsp paprika
1 clove of garlic, crushed
1 tbsp tomato purée
¼ pint (150 ml) chicken stock
¼ pint (150 ml) cider
2 tbsp cornflour
salt and pepper

Melt butter in a large, shallow pan and brown chicken joints, then add onion, chopped de-rinded bacon and garlic and cook gently for 10 minutes. Add tomato purée, stock, cider, salt and pepper, cover and cook very slowly for 1 to 1½ hours until tender. Lift chicken pieces from the pan and keep hot while you make the sauce. Blend cornflour with a little water or stock and stir into sauce in pan, bring to boil, stirring constantly and cook for 3 minutes until smooth and thickened. Taste for seasoning and pour over chicken to serve. Creamed potatoes and a green vegetable go well with this.

If preferred, white wine can be used instead of cider, and the same wine served at table. Serves 4.

Devonshire Chicken

The West country of England produces excellent cider, and this is a traditional way of cooking chicken in cider.

2 tbsp cooking oil	¾ pint (400 ml) dry cider
1 oz (25 g) butter	salt and pepper
4 chicken joints	2 tbsp Worcestershire sauce
½ lb (200 g) carrots, sliced	1 oz (25 g) flour
2 stalks celery, chopped	4 oz (100 g) frozen peas

Heat oil and butter in flameproof casserole, add chicken joints and fry quickly until browned all over. Remove and keep hot. Add prepared vegetables to casserole and fry for 5 minutes, blend in flour and cook for 1 minute, then stir in cider and sauce, bring to boil, stirring all the time. Add chicken pieces, cover and put into a moderate oven (350°F, 180°C, or No. 4) for 1 hour. Add peas and cook for a further 10 minutes. Potatoes baked in their jackets are a nice accompaniment to this dish. Serves 4.

Chicken Madeira

The sweet red wine of Madeira combines with mushrooms for this tasty dish.

6 chicken joints	1 large onion, sliced
3 oz (75 g) flour	8 oz (200 g) mushrooms, sliced
salt and pepper	1 bay leaf
3 oz (75 g) butter *or* margarine	½ pint (250 ml) Madeira wine

Put flour, salt and pepper into a paper bag and toss chicken pieces until well coated. Melt butter or margarine in a flameproof casserole, add the chicken pieces, 2 or 3 at a time, turning frequently so they brown on all sides. Remove and place on a heated plate until all the pieces are browned.

Pour off all but 2 tbsp fat from casserole, add onion and fry without browning. Return chicken to casserole and add mushrooms and bay leaf, then pour in the wine, increase the heat until it boils. Put casserole into a hot oven (450°F, 230°C or No. 8) and bake for about 30 minutes, until chicken is tender, basting half way through cooking time. If casserole looks dry add a little more wine or some chicken stock. Remove bay leaf before serving. Serves 6.

Viennese Style

4 chicken joints
3 tbsp flour
salt and pepper
½ tsp paprika
1 small egg
1 tbsp cold water

3 tbsp dried white breadcrumbs
3 tbsp grated Parmesan cheese *or* finely grated Cheddar cheese
cooking oil for frying

Put flour, salt, pepper and paprika into a strong paper bag and toss chicken joints, two at a time, until well coated. Beat egg with cold water, dip chicken joints in egg, then roll in a mixture of crumbs and half the grated cheese, pressing the coating on firmly and evenly. Leave for at least 30 minutes.

Heat cooking oil to a depth of ½-inch (or 1 cm) in a shallow frying pan and when hot fry the prepared joints, turning at intervals to brown on all sides. Reduce heat and continue frying gently for a further 20 minutes or until cooked through and crisp, but do not allow to become dry. Drain well before serving.

Leg and thigh pieces need longer cooking than wing and breast pieces. These are good served with Mixed Herb Sauce, page 145. Serves 4.

Malayan Spiced Chicken

Serve this savoury chicken over rice.

6 chicken thigh joints
bouquet garni
1 small onion, sliced
1 carrot, peeled and sliced
salt and pepper

1 oz (25 g) butter
1 tsp curry powder
1 tbsp chutney, chopped fine
squeeze of lemon juice
1 clove garlic, crushed

Add bouquet garni, onion, carrot and salt to 1 pint (500 ml) boiling water, add chicken pieces and simmer for 20 to 30 minutes. Allow to cool in the liquid, remove and drain well.

Blend together the last five ingredients to a paste, spread over the chicken pieces and leave in a cool place for 15 minutes. Place under a moderately hot grill until crisp and golden brown, turning to brown evenly on all sides.

These are also good served cold with salad, or to pack for a picnic lunch. Serves 6.

Baked Chicken and Pineapple

Either a whole chicken cut into serving pieces or ready-cut pieces can be used for this simple dish.

6 chicken pieces	salt and pepper
cooking oil	½ tsp dry mustard
flour	6 pineapple slices

Wash chicken pieces and dry well, using a pastry brush, coat pieces with oil, then drop pieces, one at a time, into a strong paper bag containing flour, salt, pepper and mustard, and toss until well coated.

Using a baking dish large enough for chicken pieces to be arranged in a single layer, brush dish with oil, and add a thin layer of oil to bottom of dish, then arrange chicken pieces on top. Place in a very hot oven (450°F, 230°C, or No. 8) for 25 to 30 minutes, turning chicken once or twice to brown evenly on all sides, brushing over with more oil if necessary.

While chicken is cooking brush pineapple slices over with a little oil or butter and put into oven to brown lightly on both sides. When chicken is crisp and golden and tender when pricked with a skewer, remove from oven and place each piece on a slice of pineapple to serve. Creamed sweetcorn is a good addition to this dish. Serves 6.

Honeyed Drumsticks

The chicken takes on a barbecue taste without having to use a barbecue in this dish. Thighs can be used if preferred.

2 oz (50 g) butter	2 tbsp tomato ketchup
1 large onion, chopped fine	14 oz (396 g) can peeled tomatoes
1 clove of garlic, crushed	salt and pepper
3 tbsp clear honey	few sprigs parsley and thyme
3 tbsp vinegar	6 chicken drumsticks
2 tbsp Worcestershire sauce	1 oz (25 g) flour

Melt butter in a saucepan and cook onion and garlic until soft. Add honey, vinegar, sauce, ketchup and chopped tomatoes, herbs, and the juice from the can. Cover and simmer gently for 15 minutes.

Toss drumsticks in flour, salt and pepper and arrange in a baking dish, brush over with sauce and cook in moderate oven (375°F, 190°C or No. 5) for 30 minutes, turning once. Add remainder of sauce and raise heat of oven until chicken is cooked. Serve with a green salad, either hot or cold. Serves 6.

Walnut and Chicken Loaf

This is a useful and tasty loaf which can be served either hot or cold, and any leftover would make good sandwiches for a snack. Either a whole chicken or chicken pieces can be used.

1½ lb (700 g) chicken meat, boneless	2 eggs
	salt and pepper
¾ cup milk	2 tsp Worcestershire sauce
1 medium onion	½ cup chopped walnuts
1 large carrot	½ cup finely chopped celery
1½ cup soft white breadcrumbs	2 chicken breasts
2 tbsp melted butter	

Cut chicken meat from bones, putting aside the two chicken breasts. If a whole bird has been used, add chopped liver to the chicken meat and make stock from the remainder of giblets.

Put chicken meat, onion, carrot and chicken liver through the coarse blade of a mincer. Turn the breadcrumbs in the melted butter and mix with the chicken, then add lightly beaten eggs, milk, sauce, salt and pepper, mixing all very well together.

Grease a loaf tin and place half the chicken mixture into the tin. Slice the chicken breasts into 6 slices (this is best done if breasts are chilled) and arrange on top of the chicken mixture, sprinkle with celery and walnuts and cover with remainder of chicken mixture, packing lightly and evenly. Bake in a moderate oven (350°F, 180°C or No. 4) for about 1 hour or until cooked through.

Remove from oven and stand for a few minutes before turning out on to a heated serving dish. Serve hot with potatoes baked in their jackets and a green vegetable or cold with salad.

If chicken pieces have been used and no chicken breasts are available, cut pieces from the upper thighs, flatten them with a rolling pin and use as directed for the breast pieces.

If you would like a sauce with your chicken loaf the giblets and carcase could be boiled up for stock, and then thickened with a little flour. Add chopped celery leaves or chopped parsley for colour and flavour. Serves 6.

Chicken and Almond Casserole

3 lb (1·3 kg) chicken pieces
few sprigs thyme and parsley
1 bay leaf
1 large onion, chopped
2 cups chopped celery
salt and pepper

½ cup blanched, sliced almonds
1½ tbsp butter *or* bacon fat
2 tbsp flour
1 cup strained chicken stock
½ cup top milk or cream

Place chicken in large saucepan with herbs and just cover with boiling, salted water. Simmer gently for about 1 hour or until bird is nearly cooked. Cool slightly and cut meat from bones, cutting it into neat dice, then drop into a paper bag with flour seasoned with salt and pepper until well coated.

Melt fat in a thick pan and fry onion, celery and almonds until lightly browned, stirring frequently with a fork. Remove with a slotted spoon, and place in a greased ovenproof casserole. Brown chicken pieces in the same pan, adding a little more fat if necessary, and keep turning chicken until golden. Add to vegetables in casserole. Stir seasoned flour into fat in pan, cook for a minute, then stir in 1 cup strained stock and top milk and bring to boil, stirring all the time until mixture thickens. Taste for seasoning and pour over chicken in casserole. Cover and cook in moderate oven (350°F, 180°C or No. 4) for 25 to 30 minutes, until chicken is quite tender.

This can be served over cooked rice, or instead of putting into a casserole the mixture can be divided between 6 ovenproof ramekins, covered with foil and baked as above. Serve with a mixed side salad. Serves 6.

Provençal Casserole

A variation on the previous recipe.

Prepare chicken in the same manner up to where it is coated in seasoned flour. Make the sauce with:

4 ripe tomatoes, peeled
1 large green pepper
4 oz (100 g) mushrooms
1 clove of garlic, crushed

2 oz bacon, cubed
½ cup white wine *or* stock
salt and pepper
1 tbsp chopped parsley

Fry the bacon in a little bacon fat, remove from pan and add chicken, turning in the fat until browned. Pour off any extra fat and add chopped mushrooms, sliced tomatoes and seeded and sliced pepper with the garlic, wine or stock. Cover and cook for 25 minutes, until chicken is tender. Serve over rice. Serves 6.

Chicken Chop Suey

In the Cantonese dialect 'Chop Suey' means odds and ends, and the story of the origin of this dish, which is now known everywhere there is a Chinese restaurant, is worth repeating.

In the goldfields of California in the early days there were many cafés opened by Chinese, and one evening three hungry miners came in demanding food, long after the café had closed. They made such a fuss that the cook went into the kitchen to see what was available, and in desperation he put all the leftovers into a pan and heated them up. The men enjoyed this so much they asked the name, and the Cantonese cook told them 'Chop Suey', as indeed it was. So a new dish was born, and it has been served in many variations in Chinese restaurants ever since. This is one version I can recommend—not made with leftovers.

1 lb (400 g) chicken, cut from the bone
¾ cup shredded, toasted almonds
2 tbsp cooking oil
8 oz (200 g) mushrooms, sliced
½ cup chicken stock
2 cup sliced celery
1 cup fresh green peas
1 tsp salt
1 tbsp cornflour
2 tsp soya sauce
½ cup cold water
¼ cup sliced spring onions
1½ cups rice
extra soya sauce

Cut chicken into dice. Using a large shallow pan with a lid, fry the chicken pieces in the hot oil for 20 minutes, stirring frequently until lightly browned. Add sliced mushrooms and fry for 3 minutes, then add celery, peas and hot chicken stock, bring to boil, cover and simmer until vegetables are tender but still crisp, about 10 minutes.

Blend soya sauce and water with cornflour and stir slowly into chicken mixture, stirring until mixture boils and thickens. Cook for 2 minutes and taste for seasoning.

While chicken is cooking, boil rice in plenty of boiling, salted water for 12 to 15 minutes until tender, then drain and run boiling water over it, draining well again and tossing with a fork to separate grains. Arrange in a ring on a heated dish, pour chicken mixture into the rice ring and garnish with the toasted almonds and sliced spring onions. Serve soya sauce separately. Serves 6.

Poulet aux Crevettes

Each year in Ostend on the Belgian Channel coast they arrange a Fête de Crevettes, or a festival of the shrimps, which dates back to the days when fishermen would trawl for shrimps on horseback. Shrimps are served in many ways in the excellent restaurants along this coast, and this is one of the most popular dishes on festival days or any other day.

4 lb (1·8 kg) chicken, cut into pieces	½ pint (250 ml) dry white wine
salt and pepper	1 tsp dried thyme
2 tbsp cooking oil	10 oz (250 g) shrimps, peeled
1 clove of garlic, crushed	1 tsp lemon juice
small piece fresh root ginger	1 tsp cornflour
3 shallots *or* spring onions, chopped	

Rub salt and pepper into chicken pieces and leave for a few minutes. Heat oil in a large flameproof casserole, add the chicken pieces and cook for 8 to 10 minutes, turning frequently until browned all over. Remove from casserole and put aside.

Add garlic, ginger and shallots to the oil in casserole and cook, stirring frequently until shallots are soft but not browned. Return chicken pieces to casserole, add marjoram and wine and bring to the boil. Cover casserole and simmer gently for 45 to 50 minutes or until chicken is tender. Add shrimps to casserole, cover and cook for a further 5 minutes, then carefully transfer chicken pieces to a heated dish and keep warm.

Dissolve cornflour with 1 tbsp wine or stock. Add lemon juice to casserole and bring to the boil, then stir in blended cornflour and cook, stirring constantly, until sauce has thickened. Pour this sauce over the chicken pieces. Serve with plain boiled rice or egg noodles, with a mixed green salad.

Prawns may be used instead of shrimps if preferred. Serves 6.

Chicken with Artichoke Hearts

For those who do not like shellfish, the previous recipe can be made with canned artichoke hearts added instead of the shrimps. The ginger should be omitted, and the artichokes added after the sauce has thickened, then just heated through.

Chicken Curry Honolulu

Brilliant sunshine, surf at Waikiki beach, hotels of great luxury, the lovely scent of the flower leis hung around the neck of every new arrival, and interesting combinations of food—these are my memories of Honolulu. I was fortunate I could bring home some recipes of those dishes I had enjoyed, and this curry is one of them.

You will find this a useful dish for occasions when dinner might have to be delayed, as it improves with slow cooking, but do not allow it to get dry. Care should be taken to use a casserole large enough to allow for the swelling of the rice as it cooks.

2½ to 3 cups cooked, diced chicken
2 tbsp butter *or* margarine
1 medium onion, chopped
1 cooking apple, peeled and chopped
1 cup canned pineapple juice

3 cups chicken stock
1 bay leaf
1 tbsp fruit chutney
3 to 4 tsp curry powder
salt and pepper
1 cup long-grain rice
4 slices canned pineapple

Melt butter in a saucepan and cook onion and apple until soft, but do not allow to brown. Stir in chutney, curry powder and pineapple juice and cook for 5 minutes, stirring at intervals. Add chicken stock and heat just to boiling.

Wash rice well, and drain.

Put one-third of the curry sauce into a large, greased casserole, add half the chicken, half the rice, two slices of pineapple, chopped into pieces, then more sauce. Repeat these layers. Place a piece of buttered paper or foil on top, then the lid of the casserole and bake in a moderate oven (350°F, 180°C or No. 4) for 40 minutes, or until rice is cooked. If necessary, reduce heat and add more chicken stock if meal is to be delayed.

For a special occasion serve the curry with bananas baked in a little butter in the oven at the same time as the curry, turning them half-way through cooking time. Also with side dishes of grated coconut, shelled peanuts, sliced hard-boiled eggs, lemon wedges dipped in paprika and extra chutney. Serves 6.

Pacific Coconut Bake

This is a rather spectacular dish which also comes from the Hawaiian Islands, and something to impress your friends next time you have a dinner party. But first, make sure fresh coconuts are available when you want to make up this dish.

6 fresh coconuts
2½ lb (1·1 kg) chicken, whole *or* in pieces
6 rashers bacon
3 ears of fresh corn
3 medium onions, sliced
1½ cups chopped green pepper
1 clove of garlic
6 small tomatoes, peeled
salt, pepper, and cayenne
1 tbsp cooking oil

With a nail or skewer, puncture three holes in the 'eyes' at one end of each coconut, and drain off the milk. (This can be used for a curry another day). From the punctured end of each coconut saw off a slice of shell to make a lid, removing the coconut meat from each lid in one piece, if possible. Grate this coconut meat on a coarse grater and put aside.

In a large frying pan heat the oil and fry the diced bacon until crisp. Pour off all but 1 tbsp oil and bacon fat from the pan. Add the corn scraped from the cobs, or if fresh corn is not available use canned sweet corn, well drained, the sliced onions, green pepper and finely chopped garlic, and 1 tbsp of the grated coconut. Fry all together, turning at intervals with a fork, until onion is tender, but do not allow mixture to brown. Add sliced tomatoes and the chicken which has been cut from the bones and diced, cook for 5 minutes.

Spoon this mixture into the coconut shells, which have been well drained and sprinkled with salt and pepper. Put lids in place and wrap each coconut completely in foil, fastening at the top. Place the wrapped shells in a baking dish so that they stand upright—foil can be crumpled round them to keep them in place if necessary—add one inch hot water to the dish and bake for 1 hour in a moderate oven (350°F, 180°C or No. 4). Open foil for the last 10 minutes baking time, remove lids and sprinkle chicken with remainder of grated coconut, return to oven until lightly browned on top.

If you have six individual ovenproof baking dishes or ramekins large enough to take each wrapped coconut use them instead of one large baking dish, and they can then be used to serve the chicken. To serve, unwrap foil in which they were baked, and make nests of foil on six plates to keep coconuts upright if not serving in individual dishes. Serves 6.

Agda's Fried Chicken

This is only suitable for a young chicken, or pieces may be used if not too large.

4 chicken pieces	½ cup dry white wine
salt and pepper	1 tsp onion juice (see below)
juice ½ lemon	flour
½ cup olive (*or* cooking) oil	2 tbsp finely chopped parsley

Wipe pieces, sprinkle with salt and pepper and arrange in one layer in a shallow dish. Cut onion in halves and with a sharp-pointed spoon, scrape the cut surface to obtain the juice. Mix lemon and onion juices, wine and half the oil and pour over chicken, allowing to stand for at least two hours, turning once during that time.

When ready to cook, drain well, retaining the marinade. Mix flour and parsley and coat each chicken piece well on all sides. Heat remaining oil in shallow pan and fry chicken pieces for about 15 minutes on each side, or until nicely browned and tender. Serve with grilled halved tomatoes, and the marinade which has been thickened with a little flour to make a sauce. Serves 4.

Chicken Parmesan au Gratin

4 chicken pieces	1 oz (25 g) butter
few sprigs thyme and parsley	1 oz (25 g) flour
½ cup dry white wine	3 oz (75 g) grated Parmesan cheese
1 small onion, sliced	
salt and pepper	

Cook chicken pieces with onion, herbs, salt, pepper and wine, and enough water to just cover chicken. Simmer until tender, about 45 to 60 minutes, then remove chicken and keep hot while you make the sauce. Strain stock.

Melt butter in a small saucepan, blend in flour and cook for a minute, then slowly stir in enough stock to make a fairly thick sauce. Stir until it boils, then cook for 2 minutes. Put half this sauce in a buttered ovenproof dish, arrange chicken pieces on top and sprinkle with half the cheese, add remainder of sauce and sprinkle with rest of cheese. Put into a hot oven or under the grill until sauce bubbles and cheese is a golden brown.

Serve with grilled halved tomatoes and peas. Serves 4.

Chicken Enchiladas with Chili Sauce

A recipe from Mexico, where they like their food well seasoned. This is a very useful dish as the majority of the preparations can be done the day before, which makes it very good for a dinner party.

For the chili sauce:

½ lb (200 g) cooked *or* canned tomatoes
1 small onion, chopped
1 green pepper
2 tsp butter
2 tsp cooking oil
2 tsp chili powder
1 heaped tbsp flour
¼ pint (150 ml) chicken stock
salt and pepper

Rub tomatoes through a sieve. Remove seeds and membranes from green pepper and chop small, fry with the onion in the butter and oil until soft. Mix chili powder and flour and sprinkle over onion mixture, stirring to blend, and cook for a minute, then stir in stock and sieved tomatoes, stirring continuously until sauce boils and thickens. Season to taste.

For Enchiladas:

12 pancakes, 6 inches (16 cm) across
3 cups, cooked, diced chicken meat
½ cup blanched, toasted almonds
2 tbsp chopped onion
1 tbsp chopped parsley
2 tbsp chopped celery
2 tbsp butter
½ cup chili sauce

Make the pancakes thin, but be careful not to break them. If made ahead of time stack with greaseproof paper between each pancake to keep them moist and fresh in refrigerator.

Put chicken through the mincer, or chop very fine. Chop the almonds and mix with the chicken, onion, celery and parsley and mix all together with ½ cup chili sauce. Place a heaped tablespoonful of the chicken mixture on each pancake and fold into an envelope shape. Heat butter in pan and sauté each pancake parcel, seamside-down, until crisped and golden brown. With a wide spatula or egg-slice carefully turn and brown other side. Do not cook more than two at a time, and keep hot while others are being cooked.

Serve on a bed of cooked rice, with remainder of chili sauce poured over the top.

The chili sauce is also very good served over plain fried chicken pieces, accompanied by canned sweet corn tossed in butter. Serves 6.

Gruyère Surprise Packet

A Swiss dish which comes as a surprise packet wrapped in foil.

6 chicken thighs
4 oz (100 g) butter
2 tbsp finely chopped chives
  or spring onions
salt and pepper to taste

½ cup thinly sliced carrots
½ cup thinly sliced celery
1 tbsp chopped parsley
6 slices Gruyère cheese
cooking foil

Cut thick aluminium foil into six 12 inch (32 cm) squares. Mix chives with butter, blending well together, and stand for 30 minutes. Spread each foil square with a little chive butter and rub each chicken piece with the butter. Place a chicken piece in the centre of each square, sprinkle with salt and pepper, top with carrot, celery, parsley and top that with a piece of cheese to just cover chicken. Bring the foil up and over and seal with a double fold, then seal each end firmly. Place the packets in a shallow baking dish in one layer and bake for 45 minutes in a hot oven (450°F, 230°C or No. 8). Unwrap one parcel to make sure chicken is cooked, if not seal firmly and return to oven.

Bake potatoes in their jackets in the oven at the same time, placing on the bottom shelf.

Serve chicken packets in the foil on heated plates, opening each one from the top at the last minute.

Chicken breasts can be cooked in the same way, but need a lower heat. Serves 6.

Coolangatta Chicken

Delicious pineapples are grown in the north of Australia, and this is one way housewives make use of them in cooking.

Allow one chicken piece and one slice of pineapple for each serve. Fry chicken pieces in butter on both sides, and when cooked through and golden brown, put aside and keep hot.

In the same pan fry the pineapple slices on both sides, then remove and keep hot with the chicken. Blend 2 tbsp flour with the butter in the pan, then stir in 2 cups unsweetened pineapple juice, stirring until gravy has thickened. Season with salt, pepper and 1 tsp lemon juice and cook for 3 or 4 minutes stirring occasionally.

Place each chicken piece on a slice of pineapple and serve gravy separately. Serve with rice or mashed potatoes and peas.

Country-Style Grilled Chicken

With young chickens, grilling is one of the best methods of cooking and takes only 25 to 30 minutes. The bird should be cut into quarters—or chicken pieces can be used if preferred—but it should be noted that the chicken must be kept well basted with either melted butter, bacon fat or oil at frequent intervals while cooking. Grill slowly, with the chicken about 4 to 5 inches (10 to 14 cm) below the heat, which should not be too fierce.

$2\frac{1}{2}$ lb (1·1 kg) chicken *or* 4 chicken pieces
half a lemon
2 oz (50 g) butter *or* margarine
salt and pepper
few sprigs fresh thyme *or* $\frac{1}{2}$ tsp dried thyme
2 rashers streaky bacon
2 oz (50 g) mushrooms, sliced

Skewer each piece of chicken as flat as possible and rub over with cut lemon. Melt butter in small pan with thyme and brush generously over the chicken pieces, season with salt and pepper. Place skin-side down in a greased grill-pan with the rack removed and cook under medium heat for 10 minutes. Turn pieces, brush over with more butter and continue grilling for another 15 minutes, brushing with more butter at intervals, and turning round, not over, at intervals. When cooked the skin should be crisp and golden and tender when leg is pierced with a skewer. You may need more butter, depending on size of the chicken pieces.

While chicken is grilling, fry the chopped bacon in the pan in which the butter was melted, then add mushrooms, turning to cook evenly, and adding a little more butter if necessary. Add juice from the halved lemon, the juices in the grill pan, season to taste and serve over the grilled chicken pieces. Serves 4.

Marinaded Grilled Chicken

As a variation on the above recipe the chicken pieces can be marinaded in either of the sauces given on page 150, then grilled as above, basting frequently with the marinade. Any marinade left over, and the juices in the grill-pan, can be added to the bacon and mushrooms to make a sauce to be poured over the chicken, or served separately as preferred.

Meal in a Pot

One big advantage of being able to buy chicken pieces is that meals for one or two people are easily prepared. This is an excellent dish for anybody living in a bed-sitting room with limited cooking facilities, as chicken and vegetables are cooked in the one saucepan.

2 chicken pieces
3 tbsp butter *or* chicken fat
1 onion, sliced
1 clove garlic, crushed
2 stalks celery, with leaves
2 tbsp chopped red *or* green pepper

2 tbsp rice
¾ pint (400 ml) chicken stock made from a cube
½ tsp mixed dried herbs
salt and pepper
½ lb (200 g) courgettes, sliced

Remove any fat which may be on the chicken pieces and melt it in 2 tbsp butter in a thick pan, removing the residue after fat has been absorbed in the butter. If there is no fat available, use 3 tbsp butter and gently fry the chicken pieces on both sides until lightly browned. Remove from pan. Fry the onion, garlic, chopped celery and peppers in the same pan, then add rice and turn frequently with a fork until butter has been absorbed.

Place chicken pieces on the rice and vegetables, add stock and herbs and bring to the boil, then cover and simmer for about 1 hour or until chicken is tender. For the last 15 minutes cooking time add the courgettes, cover and cook until tender. Taste for seasoning and serve. Serves 2.

Chicken in White Wine

This is another good dish for two which can be cooked on a single burner if necessary.

2 chicken pieces
½ cup dry white wine
1 clove garlic, crushed
4 sprigs fresh thyme *or* parsley
salt and pepper
1 onion, sliced

2 stalks celery, with leaves
1 cup chicken stock, made from a cube
2 sliced carrots
2 or 3 peeled, sliced potatoes
1 tbsp cooking oil

Put chicken in a deep dish and cover with wine, garlic, thyme or parsley, salt and pepper and leave for 30 minutes. Brown onion and chopped celery in oil, push to one side and brown drained chicken, then add stock and marinade and carrots and simmer for ¾ hour. Add sliced potatoes and cook until chicken and potatoes are tender. Serves 2.

Grosvenor House Chicken Pie

This is a recipe for an unusual chicken pie as served at Grosvenor House in London.

3½ to 4 lb (1·5 to 1·8 kg) chicken	few sprigs fresh thyme
8 slices streaky bacon	pepper
1 large onion, chopped	chicken stock
1 tbsp chopped parsley	8 oz (200 g) short pastry
1 bay leaf	1 small egg, beaten

Cut bird into 8 joints. Remove rind from bacon and stretch each rasher with the back of a knife, sprinkle with a little chopped onion, parsley and pepper and wrap bacon around each chicken joint. Put into a pie dish, add bay leaf, thyme and remainder of parsley and onion and barely cover with chicken stock (can be made with giblets from bird). Cover with short pastry, decorate top with pastry leaves and brush over with beaten egg. Bake in a moderately hot oven (375°F, 190°C or No. 5), for 1 to 1½ hours. Serves 6 to 8.

Russian Chicken Pirog

A chicken pie as served in Russia makes an interesting meal.

2 lbs (900 g) chicken pieces	4 oz (100 g) rice
1 carrot, sliced	4 hard-boiled eggs, shelled
1 onion, sliced	2 oz (50 g) butter *or* margarine
1 stalk celery, sliced	1 lb (400 g) puff pastry
salt and pepper	beaten egg yolk

Cook chicken with prepared vegetables, just covered with water until quite tender. Remove from stock and cut meat from bones into bite-size pieces. Strain the stock, and bring to the boil, then add rice and cook for 15 minutes. Strain rice well, then mix with chicken, chopped eggs and melted butter.

Line a buttered pie dish with half the pastry, add chicken mixture (if too dry add a little stock) and cover with remaining pastry, pressing edges firmly together. Prick top crust and brush over with beaten egg. Bake in a very hot oven (450°F, 230°C or No. 8) for 10 minutes, then reduce heat to moderately hot

(375°F, 190°C or No. 5) for another 25 minutes. Just before serving cut a small hole in the top pastry and add a little hot stock, then replace pastry and serve with a green vegetable. Serves 4–5.

Chicken and Oyster Pie

In New Zealand, oysters are not the luxury they have become in England, and this chicken and oyster pie is a great favourite with housewives there. If you should discover a thriving oyster bed you might like to try this recipe, but fresh mussels can be used quite successfully.

2½ lb (1·1 kg) chicken pieces, cooked
12 oysters *or* fresh cooked mussels
1 tbsp chopped parsley
1 small onion, chopped

8 oz (200 g) cooked peas
salt, pepper and cayenne
1 pint (500 ml) white sauce
  or Bechamel sauce (page 144)
rough puff pastry
beaten egg yolk

Cut meat from chicken bones into bite-size pieces. Mix with oysters or mussels (be sure they are well washed and free from grit), parsley, peas and onion and fold into sauce, seasoning to taste. Place a pie-funnel into pie dish with the chicken mixture and cover with pastry, first lining edge of dish with strips of pastry and brushing over with water, then press edges firmly together with a fork. Cut a few slits for steam to escape and brush top over with beaten egg yolk. Bake in a hot oven (450°F, 230°C or No. 8) for 15 minutes, then reduce heat to moderate (350°F, 180°C or No. 4) for a further 20 minutes. Serves 6.

Chicken Pie Pretoria

A recipe from South Africa, which has its origins in the Dutch recipes brought to that country by the wives of the early settlers.

2½ lb (1·1 kg) cooked chicken pieces
1 pint (500 ml) chicken stock
2 tbsp sago
salt and pepper

½ cup dry white wine
1 egg yolk
1 tbsp lemon juice
short pastry

Cut chicken meat from the bones into bite-size pieces and arrange in a greased pie dish. Strain stock into saucepan and bring to the boil, stir in sago and cook for 10 minutes, then stir in wine. Whip egg yolk with lemon juice and stir in a little hot stock then stir into sago mixture and cook for a few minutes, stirring all the time. Pour over chicken in the pie dish, using a pie funnel, and cover with pastry. Cut a few slits for steam to escape, decorate with pastry leaves and brush over with a little milk. Bake in hot oven (450°F, 230°C or No. 8) until pastry is golden brown. Serves 6.

North of England Pie

An old-fashioned recipe from the North of England, using a bird that is past its first youth.

2½ to 3 lb (1·1 to 1·3 kg) chicken cut into joints, cooked
4 oz (100 g) lean bacon, chopped
2 tbsp chopped parsley
peeled and sliced potatoes
chicken stock
8 oz (200 g) short pastry
little milk

Put a layer of the peeled and sliced potatoes in a greased pie dish, add half the chicken pieces and bacon, sprinkle with parsley, add another layer of potatoes, remainder of chicken, bacon and parsley and finish with a thick layer of potatoes. Add enough strained chicken stock to just cover potatoes.

Roll out pastry to cover pie dish, lining edge with strips of pastry, then seal cover in place with a fork. Cut a few slits in top, decorate with pastry leaves and brush over with milk. Bake in hot oven (450°F, 230°C or No. 8) for 40 minutes until pastry is cooked and pale golden. Serves 5–6.

Double Crust Chicken Pie

This is good served either hot or cold, and carries well for a picnic.

4 small chicken joints
4 rashers bacon
melted butter
1 lb (400 g) puff pastry
salt and pepper
3 oz (75 g) mushrooms, sliced
1 small onion, finely chopped
2 oz (50 g) butter
cream
1 egg yolk, beaten

Brush chicken joints over with melted butter and wrap each in a bacon rasher. Cook in a moderate oven for 20 minutes, then allow to cool. Roll pastry quite thin and cut into two circles, 9 inches (23 cm) and 11 inches (28 cm) in diameter. Place smaller circle on a greased baking sheet and brush edges with egg yolk. Place part-cooked chicken joints on pastry, leaving a rim around the edge. Top with mushrooms and onions and butter cut into small pieces, season to taste. Cover with larger pastry circle, pressing down between each pastry joint to make four divisions to make it easier to serve. Pinch pastry edges together, glaze with egg yolk and bake in hot oven (400°F, 200°C or No. 6) for 45 to 50 minutes. Make a few slits in pastry after it is cooked and pour in a little cream. Serves 4.

Chicken Plate Pie

Another pie which is good either hot or cold and carries well for a picnic when left on the plate in which it was baked.

2 large chicken pieces, cooked
8 oz (200 g) short pastry
4 oz (100 g) sausagemeat
salt and pepper

2 hard-boiled eggs
2 tsp chopped parsley
chicken stock
1 beaten egg or milk

Cut all the meat from the bones and cool. Roll out pastry and line a greased 8-inch (20 cm) pie-plate with a good rim. Fill centre with chicken meat, sliced eggs and sausagemeat cut into thin strips, moisten slightly with stock. Dampen edges of pastry and cover with remainder of pastry, sealing edges well with a fork. Brush over with beaten egg and cut a few slits for steam to escape, decorating with pastry leaves if liked. Stand plate on a baking tray and bake in a hot oven (400°F, 200°C or No. 6) for 40 minutes, until golden. Serves 4.

Drumsticks in Pastry

6 chicken drumsticks
3 oz (75 g) cream cheese
1 tsp mixed herbs
1 tbsp chopped parsley

1 lb (400 g) puff pastry
1 beaten egg
pepper

Mix the cream cheese with herbs, parsley and pepper. Make a small pocket in the skin of each drumstick and press in some of the cheese mixture. Roll out pastry and cut six oblongs, each large enough to enclose a drumstick. Brush round pastry edges with egg, place a drumstick in the centre of each oblong of pastry and pinch edges together to seal firmly and enclose the chicken legs. Place on greased baking sheet and glaze pastry by brushing over with beaten egg. Bake in a hot oven (400°F, 200°C or No. 6) for 20 minutes, then reduce heat to moderate (350°F, 180°C or No. 4) for a further 35 minutes. Serve hot or cold.

This recipe can also be followed using chicken breasts, in which case they will not need to be baked for quite so long. Serves 6.

Honeyed Chicken Legs

Leaving the chicken legs in a piquant marinade for some hours or overnight not only gives them a good flavour but also helps to tenderise them before cooking in a casserole.

For marinade:
2 tbsp clear honey
2 tsp lemon juice
1 tbsp tomato ketchup
2 tbsp vinegar
1 tbsp oil
1 clove garlic, crushed
1 bay leaf
salt and pepper

For chicken casserole:
4 chicken legs
1 oz (25 g) butter
2 onions, sliced
1 oz (25 g) plain flour
¼ pint (150 ml) chicken stock

Mix all ingredients for marinade and pour over chicken legs in an earthenware dish. Leave for some hours or overnight, turning occasionally.

When ready to cook, drain chicken pieces, retaining the marinade. Heat butter and fry chicken on all sides until golden then place in greased ovenproof casserole. Fry onions in same fat until transparent, then stir in flour, cooking for a minute, then add stock and marinade, bringing to the boil and stirring all the time. Pour over chicken, cover and cook in moderate oven (350°F, 180°C or No. 4) for 45 minutes or until tender. Taste for seasoning, remove bay leaf and serve over rice. Serves 4.

Honeyed Chicken Legs, Grilled

Follow the previous direction for marinading the chicken legs and when ready to cook drain them well. Place in a grill pan with the rack removed and brush over with melted butter. Cook for 10 minutes, brushing over with marinade, then turn and continue grilling under medium heat for another 10 minutes, brushing well with the marinade until legs are tender when tested with a skewer.

Serve hot arranged on a bed of rice or cold with salad. Serves 4.

Texan Chicken in a Basket

Texans are renowned for the lavishness of their hospitality, and they enjoy giving outdoor parties with the most amazing spreads of food. This is one way of cooking chicken legs for 'finger eating', when we had it accompanied by corn on the cob and bacon and banana rolls, and all kinds of salads.

6 chicken drumsticks	4 oz (100 g) dried breadcrumbs
ready-mixed American mustard	pinch mixed herbs
	2–3 oz (50 to 75 g) butter
1 egg lightly beaten	

Brush each drumstick lightly with mustard, dip in the beaten egg and then coat with the herbed breadcrumbs, being sure they are completely covered. Leave on greaseproof paper to set. When ready to cook melt the butter and dip each chicken leg into the melted butter to cover all sides. Place on a baking tray in a hot oven (450°F, 230°C or No. 8) for 25 to 30 minutes until crisp and brown and cooked through, turning once.

To make the bacon and banana rolls cut rind from bacon and wrap around a peeled banana, securing with a wooden pick. Brush over with melted butter and cook in the oven at the same time as the chicken legs, turning frequently for 15 to 20 minutes. Repeat this for required number, allowing at least one to a serve. Serves 6.

Cheesey Chicken in a Basket

Another version of the previous recipe adds 4 tbsp grated cheese to the breadcrumbs before coating the drumsticks. After coating has set for half an hour fry in deep, hot fat for 10 or 15 minutes until coating is crisp and golden and chicken is tender when tested. Drain on kitchen paper and serve hot or cold, the bone-ends protected with cutlet frills or a twist of foil, and served in a table napkin-lined basket. Good for a picnic. Serves 6.

Almond Chicken Legs
Either chicken legs or thighs can be used for this recipe.

4 chicken legs *or* thighs
1 egg, beaten

4 oz (100 g) ground almonds
2 oz (50 g) butter

Brush chicken with egg and roll in almonds, pressing well in. Place on a square of foil and pour melted butter over the top, seal firmly and bake in a fairly hot oven (400°F, 200°C or No. 6) for about 45 minutes. Serves 4.

Sweet-Sour Chicken
This is my simplified version of a very popular Chinese dish. Cooked chicken can be used if more convenient, then re-heated in the sauce.

1½ lb (700 g) boneless chicken meat
1 tbsp cooking oil
½ cup hot water
2 tbsp cornflour
1 tbsp brown sugar
¼ cup vinegar
juice 1 lemon

1 cup pineapple juice
2 tsp soya sauce
½ cup sliced green pepper
½ cup diced celery
2 tbsp chopped spring onions with green tops
20 oz (500 g) can pineapple
salt and pepper

Cut chicken into dice and turn in hot oil, stirring frequently to brown lightly on all sides. Add water, cover pan and cook gently until chicken is tender, stirring at intervals.

Blend cornflour with the pineapple juice, add vinegar, lemon juice, soya sauce and sugar and cook together until slightly thickened, stirring constantly. Pour over chicken pieces in pan and simmer for 5 minutes, add pineapple cut into pieces, onion, green pepper and celery and simmer for another 4–5 minutes. Taste for seasoning. Be careful not to overcook, as the vegetables should remain crisp. Serve over hot rice. Serves 4–5.

Hollywood Spring Chicken
Simple and delicious.

4 chicken quarters
salt and pepper
½ tsp curry powder
½ tsp dried sage

3 tbsp plain flour
2 tbsp butter *or* margarine
juice 4 oranges

Cut each chicken quarter into 2 pieces. Mix salt, pepper, sage, curry powder and flour and coat chicken pieces well on all sides, then fry in the butter until golden brown all over. Place in a flame-proof casserole and cover with orange juice, cover and cook until tender in a moderate oven (350°F, 180°C or No. 4) for about an hour. Remove chicken pieces and keep hot then boil juices in the casserole very quickly to reduce and thicken. Pour over chicken.

If obtainable, serve this with mashed sweet potatoes to which has been added 2 tsp grated orange rind. Serves 4.

Californian Chicken Bake

This is one of those dishes which are served at a 'Girls' Luncheon' in sunny California—the girls being anything from seventeen to seventy—but they like their chickens very young, and the avocados really ripe for this unusual dish.

3 large ripe avocados	salt and pepper
lemon juice	½ cup mayonnaise
2 cups cooked, diced chicken	1½ cups cornflakes
1 cup finely cut young celery	1 tbsp melted butter

Cut avocados in halves lengthwise and remove stones, peel as thinly as possible, then brush over with lemon juice to prevent discolouring. Combine chicken, celery and mayonnaise, add salt and pepper if necessary. Fill avocado halves with this mixture. Crush cornflakes and toss in melted butter, then sprinkle over the filled avocados. Place the filled halves in a greased baking dish, being careful they stay upright, and place in a moderately slow oven (325°F, 160°C or No. 3) until just heated through and topping is crisp and golden.

Serve with a tossed mixed salad. Serves 6.

Paprika Chicken

Be sure the paprika you use for this is fresh, as stale paprika takes on a musty taste which spoils the dish.

6 chicken pieces	1 large onion, sliced
1 oz (25 g) plain flour	½ lb (200 g) tomatoes, peeled
½ oz (15 g) paprika	½ pint (250 ml) sour cream *or*
salt and pepper	yogurt
4 oz (100 g) butter	chicken stock (from a cube)

Season flour with salt and pepper and coat the chicken pieces on all sides. Melt butter in a pan and fry the onions until soft but not browned. Add paprika to the pan, blending in well, then add a little stock to prevent burning. Add chicken pieces, frying lightly on both sides, then add chopped, peeled tomatoes. Cover pan and cook gently, turning occasionally, until chicken is cooked through and tender. If necessary, add a little stock to the pan.

Mix sour cream or yoghurt with remaining seasoned flour and a little stock to make a smooth cream. Add to chicken about 10 minutes before end of cooking time, re-heat but do not allow to boil, and taste for seasoning. Serve with cooked noodles. Serves 6.

Pollo Espagnole

Spanish farms produce excellent tomatoes as well as fine, juicy oranges, and here they are combined with chicken in a tasty dish.

4 chicken pieces	juice and grated rind of 1 orange
olive oil	
2 lbs (900 g) ripe tomatoes	chopped pulp of 1 orange
½ cup red wine	chicken stock (made with cube)
1 clove garlic, chopped fine	
½ oz (15 g) cornflour	salt and pepper

Place chicken pieces in a roasting pan and brush over with olive oil. Add the chopped, peeled tomatoes, garlic and wine, with salt and pepper and cook in a moderate oven (350°F, 180°C or No. 4) for 45 minutes, basting at intervals until tender. If necessary, add a little stock to the pan. When chicken is cooked, remove from pan and keep hot while you make the sauce.

Press juices in the pan through a sieve and skim as much of the fat off the top as possible. Make up to ½ pint (250 ml) with stock and heat, then stir in cornflour blended into a smooth cream with orange juice, stirring until thickened. Add chopped orange pulp (carefully remove all seeds and membranes) and grated orange rind and heat through. Serve poured over chicken. Serves 4.

Sussex Crispy Chicken

4 chicken pieces	1 clove garlic, crushed
salt and pepper	2 pkts potato crisps
3 oz (75 g) butter *or* margarine	1 oz (25 g) grated cheese

Crush potato crisps and mix with cheese. Season chicken pieces with salt and pepper. Melt fat in pan with the garlic, and dip chicken pieces into the melted butter, then coat evenly with the crushed crisps. Place in a single layer in a shallow baking tin and trickle any remaining butter over them. Bake, uncovered, for 40 minutes in a moderate oven (350°F, 180°C or No. 4) until tender and crisp. Serve hot, garnished with baked tomatoes, or cold with salad. Serves 4.

Dutch Chicken Casserole

This is a Dutch-inspired recipe I tasted in South Africa, combining Dutch cheese and South African oranges very successfully.

4 chicken thighs
3 oranges
4 thin slices Gouda cheese
1 green pepper, sliced
1 onion, chopped
8 button mushrooms

2 oz (50 g) butter *or* margarine
2 oz (50 g) plain flour
½ pint (250 ml) chicken stock
few sprigs fresh thyme
salt and pepper
watercress to garnish

Coat the chicken joints in seasoned flour, then brown in the hot butter on all sides, lower the heat and cook slowly for 10 minutes. Place in a greased ovenproof casserole and cook in a fairly hot oven (400°F, 200°C or No. 6) while you make the sauce.

In the pan in which chicken was browned sauté the mushrooms, onion and pepper until soft but not browned. Stir in remaining seasoned flour, then slowly add stock, stirring until thickened. Peel two oranges and cut flesh into pieces, retaining the juice, and squeeze juice from other orange, add all this to the sauce with the thyme, then pour over chicken joints in casserole, and continue cooking for about 30 minutes until chicken is tender.

Just before serving place the thin slices of cheese over the chicken and put casserole under a preheated grill to lightly brown the cheese. Serve garnished with watercress. Serves 4.

Fried Chicken Viennese

A popular way of cooking chicken in Vienna, serving it with some of the excellent white wine of the region.

6 chicken pieces, cooked
2 cups plain flour

4 egg whites, stiffly beaten
pinch salt

½ cup dry white wine
1 tbsp cooking oil
little extra flour
oil *or* fat for deep frying

Cut chicken into even sized joints, and dust with flour. Make a batter by sifting flour into a bowl with salt, stirring in the warmed oil, then the wine until smooth, and quickly folding in beaten egg whites. Coat chicken joints with this batter and fry in hot oil or fat until golden brown. Drain on kitchen paper and serve at once with lemon wedges sprinkled with paprika. Serves 6.

Chicken Trinidad

In the West Indies rum is used not only for drinking but also for cooking, and this is an interesting combination of flavours.

6 chicken pieces
lemon juice
2 tbsp butter *or* bacon fat
flour
salt and pepper
2 tbsp tomato paste
1 cup hot chicken stock
1 medium onion, sliced

2 tbsp currants
grated rind 2 lemons
1 tsp brown sugar
2 cups crushed pineapple
3 tbsp rum
1 tbsp blanched fried almonds
cooked rice

Rub chicken pieces over with lemon juice and leave for half an hour. Coat lightly with flour seasoned with salt and pepper and brown on all sides in the hot fat, using a thick pan. Pour off any surplus fat and add tomato paste mixed with hot stock (can be made with a cube), onion, currants (soak for a few minutes in boiling water, then drain), lemon rind, sugar and crushed pineapple. Cover and bring to the boil, then simmer until chicken is very tender. Add the rum and cook for another 10 minutes. The sauce should be thick and the chicken almost falling off the bones.

Serve over rice and sprinkle with the chopped, fried almonds. Serves 6.

Herbed Chicken with Olives

4 chicken pieces
1 clove garlic, crushed
4 tbsp cooking oil
2 tbsp flour

1 tbsp either chopped thyme *or* tarragon
½ pint (250 ml) white wine *or* cider

1 tbsp chopped chives
1 tbsp chopped parsley
salt and pepper

¼ pint (150 ml) sour cream *or* yogurt
12 stoned black olives

Heat the oil in a large frying pan with a lid and add the garlic and chicken and fry until golden brown. Discard the garlic, and put chicken to one side. Add herbs to the pan and fry for a minute, then stir in flour and slowly stir in wine or cider, stirring continuously until it boils. Add soured cream or yogurt, olives, salt and pepper to taste and return chicken to pan. Cover and cook until chicken is tender, stirring occasionally. Serves 4.

Kentish Chicken Pudding

This is a Kentish dish dating back more than a century, and it is just as good for today's meals, especially during the winter.

10 oz (250 g) suet pastry
1 lb (400 g) chicken meat off the bones, cubed
4 oz (100 g) lean veal, cubed
flour
salt and pepper

pinch mixed herbs
1 tbsp chopped parsley
4 oz (100 g) cooked ham
chicken stock, may be made with a stock cube
2 oz (50 g) button mushrooms

Grease a pudding basin and line it with two-thirds of the suet pastry, fitting it smoothly into the basin. Add mixed herbs, salt and pepper to the flour and toss the chicken and veal pieces in a paper bag with seasoned flour until well coated. Put half the chicken and veal pieces in the pastry lined basin, sprinkle with half the parsley, add a layer of chopped ham and sliced mushrooms. Repeat these layers, making the last layer chopped ham. Add enough chicken stock to just cover filling.

Roll out remaining pastry to fit top of basin with an overlap. Brush edges with cold water, carefully fit pastry on top and pinch edges firmly together. Cover with greased paper, then with a pudding cloth or cooking foil and tie down securely. Steam in a large saucepan of boiling water for 2½ hours, making sure there is plenty of water to come two-thirds of the way up the saucepan, topping it up with boiling water as necessary. Serves 4–5.

Irish Chicken

In Ireland chicken and ham are a favourite combination, especially when cooked in the national drink, Guinness.

6 chicken joints	½ tsp dried thyme *or* marjoram
½ lb (200 g) smoked **ham**, cubed	salt and pepper
12 small mushrooms	2 pints (1 litre) Guinness *or* half Guinness and half chicken stock
1 medium onion, sliced	
1 garlic clove, crushed	cornflour

Place chicken pieces in deep saucepan with all ingredients except cornflour. Cover and bring to boil, then simmer until tender, about 1 hour. Remove chicken pieces and thicken gravy with a little blended cornflour, return to gravy and serve with creamy mashed potatoes. Serves 6.

Chicken Pilaff St Hubert

This is a rather more exotic version of the usual rice dish, using fruit with the chicken in an interesting way.

6 chicken pieces	1 tbsp red currant jelly
2 oz (50 g) butter *or* margarine	1 oz (25 g) blanched almonds
1 cup red wine *or* cider	

For pilaff:

1 medium onion, chopped	salt and pepper
8 oz (200 g) long grain rice	3 dried apple rings
2 oz (50 g) butter *or* margarine	2 oz (50 g) dried apricots
1½ pints (850 ml) chicken stock	2 oz (50 g) currants

Soak apple rings and apricots in water overnight. Cover the currants with hot water and soak for 30 minutes.

Coat the chicken pieces with butter all over and place in a single layer in a roasting tin. Add half the wine or cider and cook in a moderate oven (350°F, 180°C or No. 4) for 35 minutes, increasing heat slightly for last 5 minutes to brown nicely.

While chicken is cooking prepare the pilaff. Using a flameproof casserole melt half the butter and fry nuts until golden brown, remove with a slotted spoon and drain on paper. Add a little more butter to the casserole and fry the onion until just coloured, add rice and stir well to coat grains with the butter, then add 1 pint (500 ml) stock (may be made with cubes), and bring to boil, seasoning to taste but remember that stock is already salted. Cook rice gently over low heat until all the stock is absorbed and rice is tender, forking over once or twice.

While rice is cooking stew the apricots and apples in the water in which they were soaked, for about 10 minutes until tender. Drain and cut into pieces. Drain the currants and stir the fruit into the rice, season and dot with remaining butter. Cover with lid or foil and place in oven on lower shelf, leave for 15 minutes to dry out.

When chicken is tender remove from pan and keep hot, skim off surplus fat, then stir in remaining wine and stock and the red-currant jelly and boil quickly to make a sauce.

Serve the chicken on the rice, forking it over well to separate the grains, spoon a little sauce over each serve and sprinkle with the fried nuts. Serve remainder of sauce in a sauce boat. Serves 6.

Andorran Paella

Andorra is a friendly little country situated in the high mountains between France and Spain. The people are a mixture of the two nationalities, both languages are spoken there and you can do your shopping in both francs and pesetas. The food is a mixture from both countries, and this is the Andorra version of the popular Spanish paella.

12 oz (300 g) cooked chicken meat
1 tbsp butter *or* bacon fat
1 tbsp blanched almonds
2 rashers lean bacon, chopped
1 cup long grain rice
1 onion, chopped fine
1 clove of garlic, crushed
1 pint (500 ml) chicken stock
2 tbsp tomato paste
6 sliced mushrooms
1 tbsp chopped parsley
salt and pepper

Heat fat in a large thick frying pan and fry almonds until crisp and golden, remove and drain on kitchen paper. In the same fat fry bacon pieces and onion for 5 minutes, push to one side and add the rice, turning it frequently with a fork until it is golden.

Bring chicken stock to boil and pour over the rice, stirring well. Add remainder of ingredients, except almonds, mix well and cook over low heat until all the liquid has evaporated, stirring with a fork at intervals to prevent burning, adding a little more stock if necessary.

Serve with almonds sprinkled over the top. Serves 4–5.

Brewer's Chicken

Beer adds new flavours to chicken in this simple recipe.

4 chicken pieces	½ pint (250 ml) beer
2 tbsp butter *or* margarine	2 tbsp tomato paste
12 small white onions	1 bay leaf
salt and pepper	½ cup thin cream

Melt butter in thick pan large enough to hold chicken in one layer. Brown chicken on all sides in the butter, add the onions and cook until they turn golden, turning frequently. Mix beer and tomato paste and pour around the chicken, season to taste and add bay leaf. Cover and cook over low heat for 45 minutes, or until chicken is tender.

Skim off any surplus fat and stir in cream, re-heat without allowing to boil and serve at once. Serves 4.

Chicken Sesame

Sesame seeds, which are obtainable in specialised food shops and delicatessans, give an unusual flavour to chicken in this recipe. The chicken is first grilled and then baked, so it is necessary to use a roasting tin which will also fit under your griller before transferring to the oven.

6 chicken pieces	2 tbsp dry sherry
¼ cup melted butter	salt and pepper
flour	6 tsp sesame seeds

Brush chicken pieces over with butter on all sides, then lightly coat with flour seasoned with salt and pepper. Place on a rack in the roasting tin and grill under moderate heat for about 20 minutes, turning to brown evenly. Baste with the sherry during grilling time.

Brush chicken over with remainder of butter, sprinkle with sesame seeds and transfer to moderate oven (350°F, 180°C or No. 4), baking for about 20 minutes, or until chicken is tender when tested.

Serve with fluffy mashed potatoes, pouring gravy in the pan over chicken to serve. Serves 6.

Greek Lemon Chicken

This is an American version of a Greek dish, it probably typifies the best ideas of both countries.

4 chicken pieces	flour
2 tbsp lemon juice	1 egg
2 tbsp olive oil	fine browned breadcrumbs
salt and pepper	hot oil for deep frying
2 tbsp chopped parsley	lemon wedges

Place chicken pieces in a shallow dish. Mix together oil, lemon juice, parsley, salt and pepper and pour over chicken. Leave for about an hour, turning pieces several times.

When ready to cook drain pieces well, coat in flour then in the egg beaten with 1 tbsp water, and finally in the breadcrumbs, pressing crumbs well into the flesh. Deep fry in the hot oil until golden brown and cooked through when tested with a skewer. Drain on kitchen paper and serve at once, garnished with the lemon wedges.

Chicken drumsticks are good cooked like this also. Serves 4.

Devilled in Denmark Chicken

Odense, where I tasted this dish, is known as Hans Christian Andersen's town, a delightful place to visit. With this dish the amounts of flavouring ingredients depend on personal taste, but this is the way I enjoyed it.

4 chicken pieces	2 tsp Worcestershire sauce
2 medium onions, sliced	3 tbsp tomato ketchup
2 oz (50 g) bacon fat	salt and pepper
½ tsp paprika	1 tbsp flour
1 tsp curry powder	cooked rice
1½ cups chicken stock	

Heat bacon fat and fry the chicken pieces until golden on all sides. Push chicken to one side and fry onion, but do not allow to brown. Mix ketchup, sauce, curry powder, paprika, salt and pepper and chicken stock together and pour over chicken in the pan. Bring to the boil, cover and simmer for 30 minutes, or until chicken is tender when tested.

When chicken is cooked, remove and keep hot, and blend flour into gravy in pan, stirring all the time until it thickens. Arrange chicken on a heated serving plate, surround with a ring of fluffy cooked rice and pour sauce over the top. Serves 4.

Chicken in Cognac

A simple but very elegant way of cooking chicken as served to me at a marvellous inn not far from the town of Cognac after I had been visiting the distilleries.

2 young chickens, cut in halves	2 tbsp butter
lemon juice	½ cup cognac *or* brandy
salt and pepper	½ cup thick cream

Cut each chicken in halves and skewer them as flat as possible. Rub pieces over with lemon juice and sprinkle with salt and pepper. Heat butter in a thick, shallow pan and fry chicken pieces on both sides until golden brown. Pour cognac over chicken, cover pan and simmer until brandy is completely absorbed and chicken is tender. If necessary add a little chicken stock. When tender, pour cream over chicken pieces and heat very slowly, but do not allow to boil. Serve at once with creamy mashed potatoes and tender young peas.

Chicken pieces can be used for this if more convenient. Serves 4.

Chicken Marengo

This is a useful and tasty dish for a dinner party as it can be cooked the day before and re-heated if required, and the flavour seems to improve. It is a well-known dish which tradition has attributed to Napoleon's chef, who made it after the Battle of Marengo from any food he could find, and it proved so popular with the General that it became a standard dish when on the march—and is still popular today.

2–3½ lb (1·5 kg) chickens	1 cup white wine
6 large tomatoes	8 oz (200 g) button mushrooms
1 small tin tomato paste	24 small white pickling onions
3 tbsp cooking oil	2 oz (50 g) butter
2 tbsp flour	1 clove garlic, crushed
1½ cups chicken stock (made from giblets)	salt and pepper
	2 tbsp chopped parsley

Cut cleaned chickens into serving pieces. Heat oil in a large pan and fry pieces 3 or 4 at a time, turning to brown on all sides. Drain well and place in a large casserole (or 2 smaller casseroles). Blend flour into oil remaining in pan and brown slightly. Blend tomato paste with stock and wine, stir into pan over low heat. Add crushed garlic and peeled, chopped tomatoes and stir until sauce boils and thickens.

Heat butter in another pan and sauté the peeled onions until lightly browned, then add mushrooms and cook for a few minutes.

Add onions and mushrooms to the chicken in casserole, then pour the tomato sauce over the top. Cover closely and cook in a moderate oven (350°F, 180°C, No. 4) for 1½ hours, or until chicken is really tender. Sprinkle with parsley before serving.

If dinner is to be kept waiting, lower the heat of the oven and allow casserole to cook slowly, which will not do it any harm.

Potatoes baked in their jackets until soft, then cut in halves and the pulp mashed with plenty of butter and some chopped chives and replaced in the potato skins, are ideal with this dish. Serves 10.

Bahamas Chicken Casserole

A combination of unusual flavours makes this a tasty dish. It comes from one of the luxury beach hotels in the Bahamas, but you can enjoy it in your own home without travelling that far.

6 chicken pieces
1 clove garlic, crushed
plain flour
salt and pepper
4 oz (100 g) butter *or* oil
4 large, juicy oranges
1 tbsp brown sugar
½ tsp ground ginger
½ cup shredded coconut
1 cup orange juice
2 tbsp lemon juice
½ cup sliced, stoned black olives

Combine flour, salt and pepper in a thick bag and toss the chicken pieces, one at a time, in the flour until well coated. Heat butter or oil in a thick pan with the garlic and brown chicken pieces on all sides.

Peel the oranges, carefully removing all the white pith, and cut into ½-inch (1 cm) slices. Place half the slices in the bottom of a large ovenproof casserole and sprinkle with the mixed sugar and ginger. Arrange the chicken pieces on top of the oranges and cover with remainder of orange slices.

Combine orange and lemon juice and pour over chicken, sprinkle with the coconut and cover casserole tightly. Bake in a moderate oven (350°F, 180°C or No. 4) for 1 to 1¼ hours, depending on age of chicken, but it should be very tender when served. About 5 minutes before serving add the sliced olives.

This is best served over rice which has been tossed with some finely chopped parsley, accompanied by a mixed salad.

Another version of this dish marinades the chicken pieces overnight in the orange and lemon juice with the garlic and ground ginger. The pieces are then drained, coated with seasoned flour and browned in the butter. This is good for an older bird as the marinade helps to tenderise it. Serves 6.

Captain's Chicken

This recipe was probably brought back to the southern states of America by some 18th century sea captain who had travelled to the East Indies and enjoyed some of the dishes served there. It has been modified with time, but still retains traces of the Orient.

3 lb (1·3 kg) boiling fowl, cut into joints
plain flour
1 tsp paprika
salt and pepper
2 tbsp cooking oil
2 large onions, chopped
2 green peppers
½ cup chopped parsley
2 cups chopped, peeled tomatoes
1 tsp powdered mace
2 tsp curry powder
1 cup currants
1 cup toasted almonds
cooked rice
1 clove garlic, chopped

Cut bird into joints and drop into a bag with the flour, salt and pepper and paprika, shaking until well coated all over. Heat oil in a large pan and fry pieces until browned on all sides. Remove from pan and keep hot.

Remove seeds and membranes from green peppers and slice fairly thin. In the same pan fry the onions, garlic, peppers and parsley, turning to cook evenly for 5 or 6 minutes. Add tomatoes, cover and cook all together over low heat for 15 minutes, stirring occasionally, and add spices.

Arrange chicken pieces in a large ovenproof casserole and pour sauce over them, cover and bake in a slow oven (325°F, 160°C or No. 3) for 1½ to 2 hours or until quite tender. Add currants, which have been soaked in hot water for 10 minutes and then drained, about 30 minutes before cooking time is completed.

Almonds should be blanched in boiling water, dried and split lengthwise, then toasted in the oven in a little butter until golden. Drain on kitchen paper.

Arrange rice on a heated platter in a ring, serve chicken in the middle and sprinkle almonds over the top. Serves 6.

Chicken and Macaroni Pudding

An unusual dish from Helsinki in Finland, where it is served with cranberries for a good combination of flavour and colour.

2 large chicken pieces, cooked
8 oz (200 g) macaroni
1 medium onion, chopped
½ cup chicken stock
2 tbsp grated cheese

2 eggs, beaten lightly
salt and pepper
2 tbsp butter *or* margarine
2 cups of milk
2 tbsp soft breadcrumbs

Cut meat from the bones of the chicken into neat dice (there should be at least 12 oz or 300 g). Cook macaroni in boiling, salted water for 10 minutes, then drain and rinse with hot water and drain again. Heat 1 tbsp butter in a pan and fry the onion without browning, then add chicken and turn in the butter for a few minutes, stirring with a fork. Add stock and season to taste.

Place ⅓ of the cooked macaroni in a greased ovenproof casserole, then ½ the chicken mixture, repeating these layers and finishing with a layer of macaroni. Beat eggs lightly, then add milk with a sprinkle of salt and pour over macaroni and chicken layers. Mix breadcrumbs and cheese together and sprinkle over the top, then dot with remaining butter in pieces. Bake in a moderate oven (350°F, 180°C or No. 4) for 35 to 40 minutes or until set through when tested with a knife. Serves 4–5.

Spiced Chicken with Mushrooms

6 pieces chicken
4 oz (100 g) butter
1 clove garlic, crushed
1 tsp cayenne pepper

1 tsp ground cumin
1 tsp ground turmeric
1 tsp ground coriander
12 flat mushrooms, peeled

Blend garlic and spices with the butter and leave for 10 minutes. Spread spiced butter over the chicken joints as evenly as possible and leave for an hour in refrigerator.

When ready to cook arrange the mushrooms in the bottom of a grill pan with the rack in place. Lay chicken pieces, fleshy-side down on grill rack and grill under fairly high heat, turning several times, until juices run clear when pierced with a skewer, and chicken is tender. Remove from grill and keep hot while mushrooms are cooked under high heat for a few minutes, adding a little extra butter if necessary.

Serve chicken pieces with mashed potatoes, garnish with the mushrooms and pour juices from the pan over the chicken. Serves 6.

Chicken and Prawn Pilaff

2 tbsp oil	8 oz (200 g) Patna rice
1 large onion, sliced	3 large tomatoes, peeled
4 rashers streaky bacon, chopped	4 oz (100 g) peeled prawns *or* shrimps
2 oz (50 g) mushrooms, sliced	8 oz (200 g) packet frozen peas
1 pint (500 ml) chicken stock	4 chicken thighs, cooked
	salt and pepper

Heat oil in a large frying pan and fry onion and bacon until soft but not browned. Add mushrooms and cook for 2 minutes, then push to one side and add rice, frying for 2 or 3 minutes, stirring well with a fork. Pour in hot stock, bring to boil and simmer for 15 minutes until rice is tender, stirring at intervals. Add the peas and tomatoes and continue cooking until peas are cooked, then add prawns or shrimps, turning into mixture with a fork. By this time the stock should all have been absorbed and the mixture dry. Re-heat chicken pieces and serve on top of the pilaff. Serves 4.

Louisiana Chicken

A recipe which is not for those counting their calories, like most of the dishes served in this fascinating State of the USA, but the food is certainly deliciously rich.

4 chicken pieces	4 rashers streaky bacon, chopped
oil	
flour	1 cup cream
salt and pepper	4 bananas, peeled
	butter

Brush chicken pieces over with oil, then coat with flour seasoned with salt and pepper. Add a little oil to a thick pan and fry bacon pieces, then add chicken pieces and fry gently until browned on all sides. Add half the cream and cook for about 5 minutes, when the cream should have thickened, add remainder of cream, cover pan and simmer for 25 minutes.

While chicken is cooking, slice the bananas lengthwise and fry very gently in a little butter, then remove and drain. When chicken is tender, arrange in a heated serving dish, surround with the bananas and pour cream sauce from the pan over the top.

Either sweet corn or fried, halved tomatoes are good to serve with this. Serves 4.

Russian Spring Chicken

Use tart cooking apples for this dish, and cider can be used instead of the wine if preferred, although a Russian cook would use some of their own fruity white wine.

4 chicken pieces	1 lb (400 g) cooking apples
flour	$\frac{1}{2}$ pint (250 ml) chicken stock
salt and pepper	$\frac{1}{4}$ pint (150 ml) white wine
2 tbsp butter	pinch ground cinnamon

Using a flameproof casserole heat the butter. Toss chicken pieces in flour seasoned with salt and pepper, then fry in the hot butter until golden brown on all sides. Add peeled, cored and sliced apples around the chicken, then pour in mixed wine and chicken stock. Cover and put into a moderate oven (350°F, 180°C or No. 4) until chicken is tender, about 45 to 50 minutes. Serve over cooked noodles. Serves 4

Chicken Maryland

This is one of the best known American chicken dishes.

4 chicken joints, cooked	browned breadcrumbs
flour	4 bananas
salt, pepper and cayenne	lemon juice
2 eggs	fat *or* oil for frying
4 tbsp milk	sweet corn

Remove skin from the cooked chicken pieces, then toss in a paper bag with flour, salt, pepper and cayenne until well coated. Peel bananas and cut in halves lengthwise, dip in lemon juice and then coat with seasoned flour. Beat eggs and milk together and dip chicken pieces into the mixture, drain and toss in breadcrumbs until well coated. Repeat the egg glazing and breadcrumbing. Follow same method with the bananas.

Heat sufficient fat or oil to cover the bottom of a large heavy pan to a depth of ½-inch (10 cm) and when hot add the chicken pieces and brown on all sides until crisp. Remove and drain on kitchen paper and keep hot while you cook bananas in same manner until crisp and golden. Drain well.

Serve each chicken piece accompanied by two halved bananas, and the heated sweetcorn. Fried, halved tomatoes are also good to serve with this chicken dish. Serves 4.

Spanish Chicken Ragoût

This makes a meal in a dish, needing no extras unless you serve a dish of parsleyed rice with it.

6 chicken pieces	½ cup dry sherry
salt and pepper	1 bay leaf
1½ tsp paprika	2 large potatoes, peeled
¼ cup olive oil	6 or 8 green olives
2 large onions, sliced	1 cup shelled peas
1 clove of garlic, crushed	½ sweet red pepper
1 cup chicken stock	

Combine salt, pepper and paprika and rub well into chicken pieces an hour before cooking.

Heat oil in thick pan and fry chicken pieces on all sides until golden brown, remove and keep hot while you brown the onions in the same pan, turning frequently. Add garlic, bay leaf, sherry and stock to the pan with the chicken pieces. Cover and simmer for 45 minutes, then add sliced potatoes, peas, sliced red pepper (be careful to remove all seeds) and a little more chicken stock if necessary. Cover and cook for another 15–20 minutes until chicken is tender and potatoes cooked. Add olives, taste for seasoning and serve. Serves 6.

Lemon-Garlic Chicken Parcels

4 chicken joints	2 tbsp lemon juice
1 tsp paprika	2 tsp grated lemon rind
1 clove garlic, chopped	½ tsp dried thyme
2 tsp soya sauce	pepper

Place chicken joints in a shallow earthenware dish. Combine remainder of ingredients and pour over chicken, leaving in a cool place for several hours.

When ready to cook cut four squares of foil large enough to take each chicken piece and rub with a little oil. Place a chicken piece on each square, turning up the edges to contain the marinade, which should be divided between the four squares. Seal each parcel well and place on an oven tray, put into a fairly moderate oven (375°F, 190°C or No. 5) for about an hour, then open to see if chicken is cooked. If necessary return to oven for a little longer, opening up each parcel to allow chicken to brown slightly.

Bake potatoes in their jackets in the oven at the same time as an accompaniment to the chicken. Serves 4.

Herby Chicken Pie

A West Country pie combining fresh green vegetables with chicken, which needs no other accompaniment.

3 chicken pieces, cooked	1 oz (25 g) chopped watercress
½ lb (200 g) lean, unsmoked bacon rashers	1 tbsp chopped parsley
	3 eggs
1 lb (400 g) finely chopped leeks	salt and pepper
	¼ pint (150 ml) chicken stock
½ lb (200 g) finely chopped spinach	½ lb (200 g) short pastry

Line an ovenproof pie dish with half the bacon rashers, rinds removed, then add chicken cut in fairly large pieces off the bone, then the mixed greens, seasoning to taste. Beat 2 eggs with the stock and pour over vegetables, arrange remaining bacon rashers on top, then cover with the rolled-out pastry, sealing well around the edges. Brush over with the remaining beaten egg, decorate with pastry leaves and bake in a hot oven (400°F, 200°C or No. 6) until pastry is golden brown. Serves 6.

The Devil's Grilled Chicken

This is only for those who enjoy highly seasoned foods, and appropriately I obtained this recipe in Dijon where such excellent French mustard comes from.

2 spring chickens, about
 2½ lb (1·1 kg) each
3 oz (75 g) butter
2 tbsp oil
4 tbsp Dijon mustard
salt and pepper
pinch cayenne pepper
3 tbsp chopped shallots *or*
 spring onions
½ tsp dried mixed herbs
2 cups soft white breadcrumbs

Cut chickens into quarters. Melt butter and oil together and paint over the chickens on both sides. Arrange pieces, skin side down, in the bottom of a grilling pan without the rack. Grill 10 minutes on each side, basting frequently with the butter and oil mixture, until lightly browned.

Mix together mustard, shallots, herbs and seasonings, remove chicken from griller and add a little of the basting juices in the pan to the mustard mixture, mixing well. Brush this over the chicken pieces, then roll in breadcrumbs, pressing crumbs well in to coat chicken evenly. Stand on rack in grill pan, pour remainder of basting juices over them and brown slowly for 10 minutes, turn and grill another 10 minutes, basting well. Test a leg to make sure chicken is cooked. Serves 6.

Flaming Chicken with Cherries

To surprise some special friends with a really spectacular dish make this one with chicken combined with black cherries which you flame at the table before serving.

6 chicken pieces, cooked
1 large can black cherries
1 cup dry red wine
¼ cup cherry juice
1 tbsp cornflour
2 tbsp butter or oil
salt and pepper
½ cup Kirsch or brandy

The chicken pieces should be cooked until just tender, but do not overcook so they fall to pieces. This can be done the previous day if more convenient, and stored, covered, in refrigerator.

When ready to cook, heat butter or oil—or a mixture of both—in a thick frying pan and fry chicken pieces on all sides until golden and well cooked through. Transfer to a flameproof casserole, draining pieces well on kitchen paper, and keep hot while you make the sauce.

Stone the cherries and heat in the wine, adding cherry juice to make up to 1 pint (500 ml). Blend cornflour with the ¼ cup cherry juice and stir into the cherries in wine, stirring until thick and clear, then cook for 2 minutes. Pour at once over the chicken pieces, cover and bring to the table. Put Kirsch or brandy into a metal ladle and heat slightly, set alight and pour over the chicken. When flames have died down serve immediately. Serves 6.

Minted Chicken Grill
A very young chicken gains new flavours by being marinaded.

2 lb (900 g) chicken
small can pear halves
½ cup cider
1 tsp soya sauce
dash of cayenne pepper

2 oz (50 g) butter
2 or 3 sprigs fresh mint, chopped
cornflour

Cut chicken into halves through the breastbone, trim wing tips and flatten chicken as much as possible. Place in a shallow dish. Drain syrup from can of pears and mix with soya sauce, cider, and cayenne pepper, then pour over chicken halves. Leave for several hours, turning once. Drain chicken and brush over with butter, then place under medium griller and grill gently for 10 or 12 minutes, turning to cook other side and basting with butter. Heat marinade and thicken with cornflour, heat pear halves in marinade and sprinkle with mint. Serve around chicken. Serves 2–3.

Chicken Paella
This is a somewhat simplified version of the traditional Spanish paella which would be a very good dish for a dinner party.

6 small chicken pieces
½ lemon
3 tbsp olive oil
1 lb (400 g) tomatoes, peeled
1 clove of garlic, crushed
1 green pepper, de-seeded

salt and pepper
pinch saffron
8 oz (200 g) long grain rice
6 oz (150 g) shelled prawns
6 artichoke hearts (optional)
1 pint (500 ml) water *or* stock

Rub the chicken pieces over with the cut lemon, sprinkle with salt and pepper and leave for 15 minutes. Heat oil in a large frying pan and fry the chicken pieces on all sides until evenly browned all over. Add chopped tomatoes, sliced green pepper and garlic and cook for 2 minutes, then add water or chicken stock in which saffron has been dissolved and bring to the boil. Add the rice, season to taste, and simmer very gently until chicken is tender and rice has absorbed the liquid, about 30 minutes. It may be necessary to add more stock or water, depending on how long the chicken takes to cook.

Add the prawns and cooked artichoke hearts if using, or cooked peas could be used instead if preferred. Heat for 5 minutes, check seasoning and serve at once. Serves 6.

Chicken Mozzarella

Italian cooks combine different flavours with great effect, as in this interesting dish.

2 chicken pieces	2 flat anchovy fillets
1 oz (25 g) butter	1 tbsp Worcestershire sauce
1 clove garlic	3 oz (75 g) mozzarella cheese
2 tomatoes, peeled	2 tsp capers
1 small onion, sliced	salt and pepper
½ green pepper, seeded	chopped parsley

Fry chicken in butter on both sides until golden. Add garlic, chopped tomatoes, onion and sliced green pepper. Cover and simmer for 30 minutes. Remove lid and add sauce to pan, cover chicken pieces with sliced cheese and halved anchovy fillets. Cover and cook until cheese has melted over chicken, remove to serving dish. Put vegetables in pan through sieve, pour over chicken and sprinkle with capers and parsley. Serve at once. Serves 2.

Salads, Cold Dishes and Patés

Salads, Cold Dishes and Patés

To me there is nothing nicer on a warm day than a well made chicken salad. It can be made from leftovers, but preferably from a boiled chicken that has been left to get cold in the stock in which it was cooked (see page 30). Many people say a chicken should always have the skin removed before serving, but that is a matter of taste—I think there is quite a lot of goodness in the skin, providing all the little pin-feathers have been carefully removed before cooking.

There are so many variations of chicken salad, and every housewife has her own favourite, but chicken being such a pale meat it is important to provide good contrasts in colour to make the salad look attractive. Fortunately, salad vegetables such as tomatoes (which are really a fruit), radishes, grated raw carrots, sweet red peppers, cucumbers and herbs such as chives and parsley, even black olives or black grapes, sliced oranges and red skinned apples all combine well with chicken meat and look attractive.

Piquant Danish Salad

A tasty dressing adds piquancy to plain boiled chicken for a luncheon salad meal.

1 to 1½ lb (400 to 700 g) cooked, diced chicken
3 hard-boiled eggs
1 tbsp freshly grated horseradish
1 tbsp white vinegar
6 tbsp whipped cream
1 tbsp chopped chives *or* parsley
crisp lettuce leaves

Mix horseradish with vinegar. Shell and mash the eggs or put through a coarse sieve, mix with horseradish, then stir in whipped cream. Stand for at least ten minutes, then mix in the chicken. Line a bowl with lettuce leaves and pile chicken mixture in the centre. Sprinkle with chopped parsley or chives. Serve a dish of sliced tomatoes separately. Serves 4.

Potato and Chicken Ring

Another version of the above recipe is to make potato salad by boiling 1½ lb (700 g) potatoes in their skins until tender, then peeling and slicing them while still warm. Moisten with French dressing without allowing them to become soggy, then cool. Make a ring of potato salad on a serving plate and fill the ring with the Danish salad above.

Chicken Salad Geneva

Excellent asparagus is one of the fine crops grown in the fertile Rhône Valley of Switzerland, and this is a salad I enjoyed at a friend's house in Geneva when the first asparagus was in season.

4 lb (1·8 kg) boiling fowl, cut into 4
1 small onion
1 carrot
few sprigs thyme and parsley
1 tbsp lemon juice *or* white wine
1 cup diced celery
½ cup mayonnaise
2 tsp lemon juice
cooked asparagus (*or* canned if necessary)

Cook bird the day before it is to be served, also the fresh asparagus. Simmer the bird with the onion, carrot, thyme, parsley, lemon juice or wine, and add water in which asparagus was cooked, or the liquor drained from the canned tips. Add enough water to barely cover the chicken pieces, and cook until tender. Remove from stock, cut meat from the bones into neat pieces, and return bones and skin to stock in saucepan. Cover and continue to simmer stock until it is reduced by half. Strain and cool, and place in refrigerator until next day, when it should have set into a firm jelly. Skim fat from top.

When ready to serve cut chicken into dice. Add lemon juice to mayonnaise, then beat in 1 cup of jellied chicken stock, beating until mixture is smooth. Add chicken and celery and pile on lettuce leaves for individual serves. Garnish each serve with asparagus spears. Serves 6.

Stuffed Tomatoes

1 cup chopped chicken
1 cup chopped ham *or* tongue
1 cup peeled, chopped cucumber
6 large, firm tomatoes
½ cup chopped celery
salt and pepper
mayonnaise
crisp lettuce leaves

Choose tomatoes all the same size and shape. Cut a slice from the top of each and carefully hollow out each tomato with a spoon, being careful not to pierce the skin. Sprinkle insides with salt and pepper and turn upside-down to drain.

Mix chicken, ham, celery, cucumber and chopped tomato pulp (not the seeds) together and mix with just enough mayonnaise to bind mixture together lightly, then fill tomato cups. Chill until ready to serve, placing each one on a crisp lettuce leaf. Pass extra mayonnaise separately. Serves 6.

Avocado Suprêmes

These can be served as the first course for a dinner party or as a salad meal for luncheon.

Be sure the avocados are ripe by pressing gently with the palm of the hand—don't dig your fingers into them or you will leave bruises.

3 large avocados	mayonnaise
lemon juice	salt and pepper
8 oz (200 g) cooked breast of chicken	strips of sweet red pepper, fresh *or* canned
young celery heart	

Slice each avocado in halves lengthwise and remove stones. Brush over cut surfaces with lemon juice to prevent discolouring. Chill while you prepare filling.

Dice chicken and celery and mix with just enough mayonnaise to bind lightly. Season if necessary. Pile this mixture into the hollows of the avocados, set each half on a crisp lettuce leaf and garnish with strips of red pepper, or slices of stuffed olives may be used instead. Chill slightly and serve. Serves 6.

Nasturtium Salad

This salad is only for those who have nasturtiums growing in their gardens, or have obliging neighbours who can make them available, as the leaves must be small young leaves picked just before serving. But the piquant flavour they give the chicken is well worth trying. This same mixture can also be used to make hearty supper sandwiches, using brown bread and adding a few small leaves to each sandwich.

Mix equal amounts of diced chicken, diced celery and peeled, diced cooking apples together, then bind together with a little thick mayonnaise.

Arrange several washed and dried nasturtium leaves on each plate and pile the chicken mixture on top. Sprinkle with a little paprika.

Another version of this salad is made by chopping the leaves of the nasturtium quite small and adding to the chicken mixture, then serving on lettuce leaves.

Chicken Tonnato

This unusual dish is a variation on a popular Italian recipe which uses very young veal as the principal ingredient, but this version using chicken breasts or supremes is delicious for a summer dinner party. It is best to cook the chicken the day before serving, leaving only the sauce to make just before your dinner.

4 whole chicken breasts
1 pint (500 ml) chicken stock
1 onion, peeled and halved
1 stick celery
few sprigs fresh thyme and parsley
½ cup dry white wine

For the sauce:
¾ pint (400 ml) mayonnaise
7 oz can (198 g) tuna fish, drained
6 flat anchovy fillets, drained
2 tbsp lemon juice
2 tbsp capers

Garnish:
2 large ripe tomatoes, sliced
extra anchovy fillets
6 stuffed olives, halved
crisp lettuce leaves

Place chicken breasts, first skinned and boned, into a saucepan with the onion, celery, herbs, chicken stock and, if necessary, just enough water to cover, and bring to boil. Reduce heat and simmer very gently for 20 to 30 minutes, depending on size, until chicken is tender. Remove from pan and leave to cool overnight. Strain the stock and keep for a jellied soup or another dish.

About an hour before serving time make the sauce. Put tuna fish, mayonnaise, anchovy fillets, lemon juice and capers into electric blender until smooth and well combined. If a blender is not available press the mixture through a sieve. Place chicken breasts on a serving dish and spoon sauce over them, covering smoothly. Garnish with extra anchovy fillets and halved stuffed olives. Put in refrigerator until ready to serve. Garnish with lettuce leaves and sliced tomatoes just before serving. Any extra sauce can be served separately. Serves 4.

Chicken Salade Niçoise

All along the French Riviera Salade Niçoise is a classic dish for luncheon, and although it can be made with left-overs it is worth cooking the required vegetables especially to make this delicious concoction. Purists will say it must be made with tuna fish, but I prefer this version with chicken. For the dressing:

½ cup olive *or* salad oil
¼ cup wine vinegar
2 tbsp finely chopped chives
2 tbsp finely chopped parsley
1 tbsp finely chopped basil
 (if available)
salt and pepper

Place all ingredients in a screw-top jar and shake well. Leave for some hours before using.

For the salad:
4 large potatoes
1 lb green beans
2 large tomatoes, peeled
2 or 3 hard-boiled eggs
10 or 12 canned anchovy
 fillets
12 black olives
1 lb (400 g) cooked chicken
 meat, cut from the bone
crisp lettuce leaves

Cook unpeeled potatoes in boiling, salted water until tender, but they should still be quite firm. Peel and cut in fairly thick slices and while still warm pour just enough dressing over them to coat slices. Chill.

Cut beans into even lengths and cook in boiling, salted water for 10 to 15 minutes, until tender but still crisp. Cool.

When ready to serve line a large, shallow bowl with lettuce leaves, arrange a mound of potatoes in the centre and criss-cross with anchovy fillets. Cut tomatoes into wedges, shell and quarter the eggs, dice the chicken meat and arrange all these around the potatoes to make a pleasing and colourful pattern. Garnish with the olives and pour the well-shaken dressing over the top. Cover with foil or clear film and chill until ready to serve.

Sliced red and green peppers, radishes, asparagus or cress could also be used for garnishing this salad—it should look as good as it tastes.

Mayonnaise can also be served separately if desired. Serves 4–5.

Rice Medley

Serve this in a big salad bowl which has been rubbed around with a cut clove of garlic and then lined with crisp lettuce.

3 cups cooked, cold rice	1 tbsp finely chopped parsley
2 cups cooked, diced chicken	1 tbsp finely chopped chives
1 cup diced celery	1 cup grated raw carrot
1 tbsp grated onion	French dressing (page 147)
1 sweet red pepper, chopped	mayonnaise

Mix all ingredients together, except mayonnaise, and adding just enough dressing to moisten lightly without making it soggy. Be sure all seeds are removed from the red pepper before chopping. Pile into the prepared salad bowl and garnish with tomato wedges and sliced hard-boiled eggs. Serve mayonnaise separately. Serves 4–5.

Chicken & Rice Ring

A different version of the above recipe makes a delicious luncheon dish for a special occasion.

Make up the rice salad but omitting the diced chicken, and adding 1 cup cooked peas to the mixture. Pack firmly into a ring-mould after adding the French dressing and chill for at least 2 hours.

When ready to serve unmould on to a serving plate lined with small crisp lettuce leaves, fill the centre with diced chicken bound together with a little mayonnaise. Garnish with tomato wedges and quartered hard-boiled eggs.

If you only have a limited amount of chicken for this, diced cooked ham may be added to the chicken and mayonnaise. Or slices of ham could be formed into rolls and placed around the rice ring on its serving plate. Serves 4–5.

Summer Curry Salad

Another variation on the rice salad is to add 2 or 3 teaspoons of curry powder to the mayonnaise at least an hour before adding to the rice and chicken mixture. Raisins plumped in boiling water for a few minutes and well dried are a good addition to the rice mixture. Serve with chutney as a side dish. Serves 4–5.

Florida Chicken Salad

4 chicken joints, cooked	paprika
4 tbsp mayonnaise	2 oranges
2 tbsp thick cream	3 large firm tomatoes
2 tsp lemon juice	watercress

Keeping the pieces as whole as possible, remove skin and bones from the chicken and arrange them down the centre of a flat serving dish. Mix together the mayonnaise, cream and lemon juice and spoon over the chicken to make a thick coating. Sprinkle lightly with paprika and chill for half an hour.

Peel oranges and cut into thin slices, being sure all white pith is removed. Peel tomatoes and slice. Arrange alternate slices of orange and tomato all around the dish with the chicken, garnish with cress. Serves 4.

Cold Lemon Chicken

Ideal for a buffet party.

3½ to 4 lb (1·5 to 1·8 kg) chicken, poached	¼ pint (150 ml) single cream
2 egg yolks	1 lemon
	½ pint (250 ml) chicken stock

Leave chicken to cool in the stock, then remove and drain well, placing bird in a deep serving dish. Strain the stock and remove fat from the top.

Beat egg yolks with the cream then add juice of the lemon. Heat chicken stock with 2 or 3 strips of lemon peel, being careful not to cut into white pith. Pour a tablespoonful on to the cream mixture, stirring well, then pour all back into the pan with the stock, stirring all the time until sauce thickens, being careful it does not boil. Remove peel. Pour sauce over the chicken, coating it well, leave until cool then chill until ready to serve.

Garnish dish with sliced tomatoes alternated with sliced cucumbers and carve at the table. Serves 5 or 6.

Chicken and Mushroom Salad

1 lb (400 g) cooked chicken meat
½ lb (200 g) small mushrooms
French dressing
1 tbsp finely chopped chives
mayonnaise
lettuce leaves

Wash mushrooms well and slice them, then put into a basin with the chives and French dressing (page 147) and leave in a cool place for 30 minutes. When ready to serve cut chicken into bite-size pieces and toss with the drained mushrooms, add just enough mayonnaise to bind together and serve on a bed of lettuce. Serves 4–5.

Chicken Waldorf Salad

Mix together diced chicken meat, diced peeled apples and chopped walnuts. Add just enough mayonnaise to bind together and serve in lettuce cups.

Another version of this salad uses chopped celery instead of the apples, or celery can be added to the first mixture.

Chicken and Celery Mould

This can be made up in one mould or in 4 or 5 individual moulds as required. Serve on lettuce leaves.

1 packet lemon jelly
salt and pepper
2 tsp grated onion
3 tbsp vinegar
½ pint (250 ml) hot chicken stock
4 oz (100 g) grated raw carrot
4 oz (100 g) chopped celery
2 tbsp chopped sweet red pepper
8 to 10 oz (200 to 250 g) diced cooked chicken

Place jelly, onion and vinegar in measuring jug. Add stock (may be made with cube) and stir until jelly is dissolved. Make up to 1 pint (500 ml) with water. Fold in remaining ingredients and pour into wetted moulds. Chill until firm, then turn out on to lettuce and garnish with peeled, sliced tomatoes. Hand mayonnaise separately.

When home-made chicken stock is available, carefully strained and all fat removed, it can be used to make up the amount of liquid required instead of water. This gives a much richer jelly mould. Serves 4 or 5.

Chicken Salad Caracas
A delicious salad for those who like avocado.

4 cooked chicken quarters	1 tbsp orange juice
1 large orange, peeled	1 tsp lemon juice
lettuce leaves	3 tbsp olive oil
1 large avocado	salt and pepper

Peel avocado as thinly as possible, remove stone and cut flesh into chunks. Put into container of electric blender with orange and lemon juice, olive oil and salt and pepper and blend until smooth and creamy. Chill until ready to serve.

Remove skin and bones from chicken quarters, keeping them as neat as possible. Arrange crisp lettuce on four individual plates and place chicken on lettuce. Remove all white pith from orange and cut into slices. Spoon avocado sauce over chicken and garnish with halved orange slices. A few black olives go well with this salad if liked. Serves 4.

Chicken and Carrot Mousse
An unusual jellied loaf which makes a delicious summer dish.

1 tbsp chopped onion	1 cup cooked, diced chicken
1 clove garlic, crushed	1 chicken stock cube
2 fl oz (50 ml) boiling water	1 cup double cream
2 tsp gelatine	

For second layer:	pinch dried tarragon
2 tsp gelatine	¾ lb (300 g) cooked, sliced carrots
2 fl oz (50 ml) boiling water	
pinch nutmeg	2 tbsp mayonnaise
salt and pepper	

In an electric blender put the boiling water, gelatine and onion and garlic (from first half of recipe) and blend for half a minute. Add chicken meat, seasonings and chicken stock cube and blend until smooth, then add cream. Pour this mixture into a 2 pint (1 litre) loaf tin or oblong casserole and chill until set.

Wash blender container and put remaining gelatine and boiling water into container and blend for half a minute. Add carrots and mayonnaise and blend until creamy. Pour this mixture over the firmly set chicken mousse and chill until set.

When ready to serve unmould on cold serving dish and garnish with crisp lettuce hearts and tomato quarters. If liked, the top of the mousse can be garnished with a row of sliced stuffed olives. Serves 6.

Surfer's Paradise Salad

This recipe comes from one of the luxury hotels at Surfer's Paradise, on the Queensland coast of Australia, and is a delicious dish for a summer dinner party.

2 large avocados	¼ pint (150 ml) mayonnaise
2 large oranges	1 tbsp tomato paste
6 cooked breasts of chicken	2 tsp Worcestershire sauce
lemon juice	crisp lettuce leaves

Peel oranges, removing all white pith, and cut into slices. Halve avocados, remove stones and peel as thinly as possible. Cut into slices crosswise, and sprinkle with lemon juice to prevent discolouring. Put oranges and avocados in refrigerator to chill while you make the dressing.

Mix together mayonnaise, sauce and tomato paste, beating together until smooth and well mixed, stand in a cool place for 30 minutes before using.

When ready to serve place the chicken breasts in a row down the middle of a large oval serving dish, covering each one with the mayonnaise. Place a row of lettuce leaves down each side and arrange alternate slices of orange and avocado on the lettuce. Serve remainder of mayonnaise separately. Serves 6.

Chicken and Corn Salad

Substantial enough for a main dish on a summer's day, this salad looks as attractive as it tastes.

3 lb (1·3 kg) chicken, cooked	mayonnaise
6 medium tomatoes	2 hard boiled eggs
6 oz (150 g) cooked peas	crisp lettuce leaves
6 oz (150 g) canned sweetcorn	

The chicken can be roasted or boiled as preferred, but it should be quite cold before serving. Carve it into 6 neat pieces and remove the skin.

Cut a slice from the top of each tomato (they should be as near the same size as possible) and carefully hollow out the seeds and core. Season with salt and pepper and turn upside-down to drain for 5 minutes. Mix peas and sweetcorn together and divide between the six tomatoes, adding a little mayonnaise to each one. Arrange lettuce leaves on a flat serving dish and place chicken pieces alternately with the tomatoes around the dish. Garnish with sliced egg. Serve mayonnaise separately. Serves 6.

Asparagus and Chicken Mould

Something special for a summer dinner, to be made the night before and turned out and served with a colourful salad.

2 cups cooked, diced chicken	large can asparagus tips
½ pint (250 ml) chicken stock	salt and pepper
1 tbsp tarragon vinegar	mayonnaise
2 tbsp cold water	lettuce, tomatoes, cooked
1 tbsp gelatine	peas

Using a measuring jug dissolve gelatine in the cold water. Bring strained chicken stock and vinegar to near boiling and stir into dissolved gelatine. Drain the asparagus tips and add enough of the asparagus liquor to gelatine mixture to bring it up to ¾ pint (400 ml). Pour a little of the gelatine mixture into an oblong mould and chill until nearly set. Arrange half the asparagus tips in a neat layer, cover with aspic and chill until set. The aspic can be kept liquid over hot water while these layers are being set.

Arrange chicken over the asparagus layer, cover with aspic and chill until set, then cover with remaining layer of asparagus and aspic and chill until ready to serve.

Unmould on to a cold serving dish, surround with crisp lettuce cups with a spoonful of cold peas in each cup, and garnish with sliced tomatoes. Cut mould in slices to serve and pass mayonnaise separately. Serves 4–5.

Chicken and Ham Rolls with Pineapple

15 oz (425 g) can pineapple slices	1 celery heart, chopped
	chopped chives
½ lb (200 g) cooked chicken	mayonnaise
6 fairly thick slices cooked ham	crisp lettuce leaves
	tomatoes, peeled and sliced

Drain the pineapple slices well and arrange 6 slices on lettuce leaves on a serving platter. Chop the remaining pineapple, dice the chicken quite small and mix pineapple, chicken, chives and celery together, binding with a little mayonnaise. Use this mixture to fill 6 ham rolls, fastening each with wooden picks if necessary, and place a ham roll on each pineapple slice. Garnish with tomato slices and serve mayonnaise separately. Serves 6.

Chicken Salad Caprice

1 large, ripe banana	3 tbsp mayonnaise
2 tbsp lemon juice	2 tbsp cream
1 large orange	4 oz (100 g) black grapes
12 oz (300 g) cooked chicken, diced	*or* black olives
	crisp lettuce leaves

Peel and slice the banana into a bowl with the lemon juice turning until well coated. Peel orange and cut into dice, removing membranes and pips, and add to bowl with the chicken. Add cream to mayonnaise and mix lightly with chicken mixture, chill in refrigerator for about an hour.

When ready to serve, line salad bowl with crisp lettuce leaves and pile mixture in the centre. Garnish with olives or the halved and de-seeded grapes. Serves 4.

Melon Luncheon Salad

This is a salad I have enjoyed both in California and in my home country, Australia, and you can enjoy it whenever melons are obtainable. You need fairly large melons such as cantaloupes to make a good luncheon dish for four.

2 ripe melons	1 cup cold cooked rice
1 tsp curry powder	½ cup cooked, diced ham
1 cup mayonnaise	1 tbsp chopped chives
2 cups cooked, diced chicken	strips sweet red pepper

Cut melons in halves and scoop out seeds. Using a ball-scoop or a rounded teaspoon scoop out just enough balls to make 1 cupful, taking a little of the pulp from each half to make evenly hollowed-out shells. Cover shells with foil or film and place in refrigerator to chill.

Blend curry powder and chives with mayonnaise and stand for about half an hour, then mix with chicken, ham, rice, and melon balls. Chill until ready to serve, then pile into melon shells and garnish with strips of red pepper.

Using smaller melons and omitting the rice, these make an ideal starter for a dinner party, and are especially useful as they can be prepared well ahead. Serves 4.

Swedish Cold Curried Chicken

You will find this salad on many of the smorgasbord menus for which Sweden is famous, along with a varied assortment of other tasty dishes, but this is also good served for a summer meal with salad greens.

The mayonnaise should be prepared at least two hours before it is to be used to allow flavours to blend together.

¾ cup mayonnaise	1 cup peeled diced apple
2 tsp curry powder or paste	1 cup diced celery
1 tbsp lemon juice	2 tsp chopped fresh dill *or*
½ cup thick cream, whipped	chives
2–3 cups cooked, diced chicken	

Blend 1 tsp curry powder or paste into the mayonnaise, then taste before adding any more, as the curry flavour should not be too strong. Add lemon juice and more curry if needed, then fold in whipped cream and stand in a cool place for several hours.

Mix together chicken, apple, celery and herbs, and just before serving toss all together lightly with the prepared mayonnaise. Shape into a mound on a serving plate and garnish with sliced hard-boiled eggs and tomato wedges, or line a salad bowl with crisp lettuce leaves and pile the chicken mixture in the centre, garnishing with strips of sweet red peppers. Serve bowls of sliced tomatoes and sliced cucumber separately. Serves 4.

Chicken with Salsa Verde

This is a favourite way of serving cold chicken on a warm day in many houses in Italy.

4 cooked chicken pieces	3 tbsp olive oil
1 tbsp capers	2 tbsp lemon juice
1 clove of garlic	fresh chives
½ cup fresh parsley	salt and pepper to taste

Purée the capers, garlic, chives and parsley in an electric blender, or chop very finely. Slowly stir in oil and lemon juice, then season to taste. Pour over cold chicken and serve on lettuce leaves, garnished with strips of sweet red peppers.

Another version of this sauce adds 3 or 4 canned anchovy fillets to the green mixture as it is puréed, but in this case omit salt when seasoning. Serves 4.

Glazed Cold Chicken

Ideal for a buffet party or a summer dinner party.

3½ lb (1·5 kg) chicken	1 bay leaf
1 onion	salt and pepper
1½ pint (850 ml) boiling water	1 tsp curry powder

For the glaze:

2 level tsp gelatine	1 tbsp tomato ketchup
2 tbsp thick mayonnaise	½ tsp castor sugar

To garnish:

crisp lettuce	parsley
3 or 4 stuffed olives	radishes
capers	bunch watercress

Remove giblets from inside chicken and wash well. Place bird in large saucepan with giblets, onion and seasonings, add boiling water. Bring to boil, cover and simmer for 45 to 50 minutes until bird is nearly tender, but do not overcook or it will fall to pieces. Remove from heat and leave to cool in stock.

When quite cold carefully remove from stock, remove skin; break off wing tips, lower leg joints and parson's nose. Place chicken in refrigerator. Put skin and trimmings into saucepan with stock and bring to boil, then boil quickly, uncovered, for 5 minutes to reduce stock. Strain, cool and skim off fat. Measure ¼ pint (150 ml) stock into a basin, and from this take 1 tbsp and put into cup with gelatine. Stand cup in a pan of water over moderate heat and stir until gelatine is dissolved. Remove from heat. Add mayonnaise, ketchup and sugar to remaining measured stock in basin, stir in gelatine mixture and mix well. Leave in cool place until just beginning to set.

Make sure chicken is perfectly dry, then place on a wire rack over a plate. When glaze is the consistency of thick cream, take a pastry brush and brush in a thin film all over the chicken. Spoon remaining glaze over chicken, working quickly to get as smooth a surface as possible. If glaze sets too quickly place basin in hot water for a few seconds, stirring until smooth, then continue spooning over chicken.

Carefully lift chicken on to a serving dish and garnish breast with sliced olives, capers and parsley with stalks to make a flower pattern. Place a small bunch of watercress just behind tip of breastbone, and arrange lettuce cups and radishes around the bird. Chill until ready to serve. Serves 6.

Chicken Mousse

Ideal for a summer luncheon in the garden.

2 cups cooked, chopped chicken	salt and pepper to taste
2 cups thick cream	1 cup chicken stock
2 tbsp Madeira wine	2 hard-boiled eggs
1 tbsp gelatine	canned mushrooms
	lettuce cups

Put chicken through the mincer twice. Whip cream until thick then fold into chicken with the Madeira, season lightly. Soften half the gelatine in cold water, then dissolve in 3 tbsp hot chicken stock. Add to chicken mixture, mixing well. Dissolve remaining gelatine in remaining hot stock and pour a layer into bottom of mould. Chill until set, then arrange a pattern of egg slices and mushroom slices on top. Carefully add remainder of aspic and chill until firm. Fill mould with chicken mousse, chill until set then unmould on serving plate and garnish with remainder of mushrooms in lettuce cups. Serves 4–5.

Drunken Chicken

San Francisco has the largest Chinese population of any city outside China and its Chinatown is a fascinating place in which to wander, look in the shops and eat in the excellent restaurants. This unusual recipe is one which is only prepared for a special occasion, and we tasted it at a birthday party for the eldest son of the house. You might like to try it for a special occasion in your house, served cold with salad.

2 to 2½ lb (1 kg to 1·2 kg) chicken
1 tsp salt
enough dry sherry to cover chicken

Clean chicken and wash well, then truss securely. Bring water to boil in a large saucepan, add salt, then lower chicken into it and cover with lid. Remove from heat and allow to stand until water is quite cold. Remove chicken from water and dry inside and out, then place in a large bean pot or casserole with a tight-fitting lid and cover bird completely with sherry. (In China they would use rice wine). Place in refrigerator for about a week, and when ready to serve remove chicken and drain well, then cut in pieces to serve.

The sherry may be kept in refrigerator for another Drunken Chicken, or used in a casseroled chicken.

Cold Chicken and Ham Pie

Stuffed green olives add colour and flavour to this tasty cold pie, which is best served cold within 24 hours of baking. It is ideal for a picnic as it carries well if left in the tin in which it was baked.

2 large, cooked chicken joints	little milk
8 oz (200 g) cooked ham	8 stuffed olives, halved
salt, pepper and pinch dry mustard	¼ pint (150 ml) jellied chicken stock
	8 oz (200 g) short pastry

Remove meat from bones and put through coarse blade of mincer with ham, or chop finely. Place in bowl with olives, seasoning, chicken stock and mix well together.

Roll out pastry, take two-thirds and line base and sides of a 7-inch (17·5 cm) square baking tin. Spread filling over pastry and cover with remaining pastry, damping the edges and sealing firmly. Make two slits in centre of pastry. Brush over with a little milk and bake in fairly hot oven (400°F, 200°C or No. 6) for 30 minutes, then reduce heat to moderate (375°F, 190°C, No. 5) for a further hour.

Remove from oven and leave to get cold, cut in slices to serve. Serves 6–8.

Potted Chicken Spread

In the days when every country housewife had her own chickens in the backyard, this spread was a great favourite. It is still a good way of using up an old bird.

1 boiling fowl
1 bacon knuckle
1 bay leaf

pepper
butter

Soak knuckle overnight. Put fowl and bacon into saucepan and cover with boiling water. Add bay leaf and simmer until meat almost leaves the bones. Remove meat, cut layer of fat from bacon, and put chicken meat and bacon through fine blade of mincer twice. Add a little of the strained stock, season with pepper and add enough melted butter to make a good spreadable paste. Pack into small jars and put a layer of melted butter over the top.

This will keep in refrigerator for 4 or 5 weeks, and makes a good sandwich spread, or on biscuits to serve as appetizers with pre-dinner drinks.

Ham and Chicken Paté

8 oz (200 g) cooked chicken meat
10 oz (250 g) cooked ham
4 oz (100 g) butter
1 large onion, finely chopped
1 tbsp chopped parsley
2 tsp chopped fresh thyme
$\frac{1}{4}$ tsp ground mace
4 tbsp sherry
few drops Tabasco sauce

Chop chicken and ham very fine. Melt 1 oz (25 g) of butter in a frying pan and cook onion until soft, but do not brown. Add remainder of butter and allow to melt. Take pan off heat and mix in the ham and chicken until butter and onion are absorbed. Put this mixture into an electric blender with remainder of ingredients and work until smooth. Check for seasoning, then press mixture into an earthenware dish and chill in refrigerator for a couple of hours before serving.

Mixed Liver Paté

This is an unusual mixture of three kinds of liver to make a tasty paté made in an electric blender or it can be put through the fine blade of the mincer.

$\frac{1}{2}$ lb (200 g) chicken livers
$\frac{3}{4}$ lb (300 g) calf *or* lamb's liver
1 clove of garlic, crushed
1 tbsp lemon juice
2 tbsp brandy *or* sherry

¼ lb (100 g) pig's liver
2 oz (50 g) butter *or* bacon fat
1 egg, lightly beaten
salt and pepper to taste
6 slices streaky bacon
1 bay leaf

Soak liver for 5 minutes in cold water, drain and trim and chop coarsely. Fry in the fat until lightly browned, turning to cook evenly. Put liver and juices from the pan into the blender with egg, brandy, lemon juice and seasoning and blend until smooth. If your blender has only a small container it may be necessary to do this in two lots.

Line an oblong terrine or loaf tin with half the bacon slices (remove rinds), pack the liver mixture into the tin and place bay leaf on top, then cover with remainder of bacon slices. Cover with foil so that the foil overlaps the edge of the tin, then tie firmly to keep it in place. Place in a baking tin with a little water and bake in moderate oven (350°F, 180°C, or No. 4) for about 1¼ hours.

When cooked through and firm place a weight on top of foil covering and leave paté overnight. Remove bay leaf before serving. Cut in slices and serve with hot toast.

Paté Rosemary

Stuffed olives add colour and flavour to this paté.

1 large onion, chopped
1 clove of garlic, crushed
8 oz (200 g) chicken livers
8 oz (200 g) pork sausagemeat
salt and pepper to taste
5 or 6 rashers streaky bacon
2 oz (50 g) stuffed olives
good sprig fresh rosemary

Put chicken livers, onion and garlic through electric blender until smooth. Mix with sausage meat, salt and pepper. Remove rind from bacon and stretch rashers with the back of a knife. Place rosemary in bottom of a 1 lb (400 g) loaf tin, then line tin with bacon rashers on the bottom and sides. Spread half the meat mixture in the tin, arrange the olives in three rows, lengthwise, then cover with remaining meat mixture, and smooth top.

Cover with foil, place in a baking tin with at least one inch of water, and bake in a fairly moderate oven (325°F, 170°C or No. 3) for 1½ hours. Remove from oven, place a weight on top and leave to get cold. Store in refrigerator until ready to serve, cut in slices with hot toast.

Chicken Liver Spread

Spread on dry biscuits or fingers of toast this mixture makes a delicious addition to party snacks or for sandwiches.

8 oz (200 g) chicken livers	1 tbsp sherry
1 medium onion, finely chopped	1 tbsp sweet stout
3 oz (75 g) butter	salt and pepper to taste

Cook chopped onions in 2 tbsp butter until soft. Add chopped chicken livers and cook for 10 minutes, turning frequently. Remove from pan and mash livers and onion with a fork until smooth. Add sherry and stout to pan, scraping up residue in bottom of pan, then add to chicken livers, mixing well. Cool and add remainder of butter, season to taste, adding a dash of cayenne if liked.

If making in an electric blender, add onion-liver mixture after cooking, then add remainder of ingredients and blend until smooth and creamy.

Chicken Liver and Cheese Spread

Make this tasty spread in an electric blender.

½ lb (200 g) chicken livers	½ tsp curry powder
1 small onion, sliced	1 tbsp Worcestershire sauce
¼ cup chicken stock	salt and pepper
2 tbsp sherry	½ lb (200 g) cream cheese
½ tsp paprika	

Wash, trim and halve chicken livers, put into a small saucepan with the onion and chicken stock and simmer together for 5 minutes. Add sherry and seasonings and put aside to cool.

When mixture is cooled empty into blender container, cover and blend until smooth, then add cheese gradually, blending all the time, until you have a smooth mixture. Turn into a container and chill until ready to serve.

Chicken Liver Terrine

Use an oblong terrine or loaf tin in which to bake this to make it a good shape to cut in slices to serve.

¾ lb (300 g) chicken livers
2 tbsp butter *or* bacon fat
1 onion, sliced
1 clove garlic
¾ lb (300 g) pork sausage meat
2 eggs
pinch ground nutmeg
½ tsp dried thyme
salt and pepper
4 tbsp brandy *or* sherry
salt and pepper
3 tbsp flour
bacon rashers
1 bay leaf

Wash and trim chicken livers and sauté in the butter until firm, remove with a slotted spoon and cook onion and garlic in the butter for a few minutes. Allow to cool, then put chicken livers, onion and garlic through fine blade of a mincer, or put through an electric blender until just coarsely blended. Combine with all other ingredients except bacon and bay leaf, making sure it is well mixed.

Line terrine or loaf tin with overlapping rashers of rindless bacon and press mixture into it, pressing down firmly and evenly. Place bay leaf on top and cover with more bacon slices. Cover with foil tied firmly in place, stand in a baking tin with a little water and bake in a moderate oven (350°F, 180°C or No. 4) for 1 to 1½ hours until juices run clear. Remove from oven and cool for 10 minutes, then place weight on top and cool thoroughly. Refrigerate, but serve at room temperature, accompanied by slices hot toast.

Chicken Curry Spread

A simple way to use up leftover chicken as a sandwich spread.

1 cup cooked, chopped chicken
½ cup mayonnaise
1 tsp curry powder
1 tsp grated onion
1 tbsp salted peanuts
dash of cayenne pepper

Put all ingredients into container of electric blender and blend at high speed until smooth. This could also be put into 4 small pots and served as a first course with toast.

Terrine of Chicken

Ideal for a buffet party, served cold with salad, or as a first course for dinner with fingers of freshly made toast. Make this the day before it is to be served.

3½ lb (1·5 kg) chicken
1 chicken liver
¾ lb (300 g) pork sausage meat
1 small onion, chopped
finely grated rind ½ lemon
salt and black pepper
1 tbsp chopped parsley
1 beaten egg
8 rashers fatty bacon
1 bay leaf

With a sharp knife remove chicken breasts (see page 135), cut into long thin strips. Cut remaining flesh from the bones of the chicken, putting aside the carcase for stock. Put chicken meat through the fine blade of a mincer with the chicken liver and onion. Mix with the beaten egg, lemon rind, parsley and sausage meat and season to taste, remembering that bacon may be salty. Be sure the mixture is well mixed together, then stand for half an hour.

Line an ovenproof terrine or oblong loaf tin with three derinded rashers of bacon which have been stretched with the flat of a knife. Press in a layer of the chicken mixture, arrange half the sliced chicken breasts neatly on top with a rasher of bacon, then repeat these layers pressing down firmly until terrine is filled and all ingredients are used, finishing with a layer of bacon rashers. Place bay leaf on top, cover with a layer of foil tied firmly in place, stand in a baking tin with a little water and bake in a moderate oven (350°F, 180°C or No. 4) for about 2 hours. Remove from oven and cool for a few minutes, then place a weight on the top and cool thoroughly. Remove weight and store in refrigerator overnight, but serve at room temperature with hot toast.

Liver Paté with Black Olives

This rather unusual combination makes an interesting change.

4 oz (100 g) black olives
1 lb (400 g) chicken livers, halved
1 small onion, chopped
3 tbsp butter
3 tbsp bacon fat
2 tsp oil
1 clove garlic, crushed
¼ tsp each salt, pepper, paprika and grated nutmeg
1 or 2 tbsp brandy
parsley heads
extra black olives

Remove stones from olives and chop roughly. Heat bacon fat and oil together in a thick pan and fry the onion and garlic until lightly browned. Discard garlic. Add chicken livers to pan and cook until stiffened and partially cooked, about 3 minutes, turning frequently. Add seasonings, raise heat and add warmed brandy, set alight and shake pan until flames die.

Pour chicken livers and juices in pan into container of electric blender with the butter and blend until smooth. Cool mixture and mix in the chopped olives, pack into small individual pots and chill until ready to serve, or shape into a loaf on a serving plate, garnish with parsley heads and extra olives and cut in slices to serve with hot toast.

With Chicken Livers

With Chicken Livers

Chicken livers can be bought frozen in most supermarkets, and make tasty and easily cooked dishes. They are ideal for paté (see page 119) or for cooking on skewers (see page 158), for a delicious sauce over spaghetti or to serve over rice as a main course.

After thawing they should be washed well in cold water, and any greenish-looking bits cut away as these may be bitter.

Chicken Livers Jerez

This is a dish I always associate with Jerez de la Frontera, the charming town in southern Spain where the splendid sherries come from. It was served bubbling hot in dishes of brown, locally-made pottery, giving off a delectable aroma of sherry, as the first course to a wonderful dinner. (The main course was partridge, but that is another story). I brought some of the same shallow dishes home with me and always use them to serve this delicious mixture of chicken livers and mushrooms.

1 lb (400 g) chicken livers, sliced
3 tbsp butter
½ cup thinly sliced onions
6 oz (150 g) mushrooms
¼ tsp finely chopped rosemary
¼ pint (150 ml) dry sherry
2 tsp cornflour
salt and pepper

Heat butter in thick pan and sauté onions until golden brown and soft. Add sliced mushrooms and cook for a few minutes, turning frequently, then add chicken livers, rosemary and the salt and pepper. Sauté until livers are lightly browned and stiffened, turning at intervals for 2 or 3 minutes.

Blend cornflour to a cream with a little water. Add sherry to the chicken livers and bring mixture just to boiling. Stir in cornflour, stirring until mixture has thickened, then reduce heat and simmer for 2 or 3 minutes until livers are cooked.

If serving in individual dishes, divide the cooked mixture between them and put into a fairly hot oven until bubbling, then serve at once. This can also be served as the main dish for a meal over a mound of cooked rice, sprinkled with finely chopped parsley and served with lemon wedges. Serves 4.

Chicken Livers Piquant

This is a rather unusual mixture of flavours which is good served over buttered noodles. I enjoyed this dish in the Swiss town of Rapperswil, but it is probably of German origin.

1 lb chicken livers, halved
3 tbsp flour
salt and pepper
4 tbsp butter *or* margarine
2 cooking apples, peeled
1 large onion, sliced thin
1 tbsp brown sugar
noodles

Wash livers and drain well. Season flour with salt and pepper and put into a strong bag, then toss livers in it until well coated all over. Heat half the butter in a thick frying pan and sauté the livers until browned all over, about 3 minutes until stiffened, but do not overcook or they will be tough. Remove from pan and keep hot over boiling water while you fry the onion in the same pan until tender.

In another pan melt remainder of butter and fry the thinly sliced apples, turning to brown on both sides and sprinkling with sugar to glaze. Care must be taken to keep the slices intact.

While these various stages of cooking are going on cook the noodles in boiling salted water until tender, drain well and toss with a little butter. Arrange in a ring on a heated serving dish. Mix livers and onions and place in noodle ring, then garnish over the top with the glazed apples. Serve at once, accompanied by a mixed salad. Serves 4.

Chicken Livers with Tomatoes

This is a very useful recipe for two people, quick to make.

1 medium onion, chopped
½ green pepper, sliced
½ lb (200 g) chicken livers
1 tbsp oil
2 tsp butter
4 tomatoes, peeled and chopped
3 or 4 sprigs fresh thyme
2 tbsp sherry
salt and pepper
4 tbsp long-grain rice

Wash livers and cut in halves. Heat oil and butter in a thick pan and fry onion and green pepper until tender. Push to one side of pan and cook chicken livers for 2 minutes, turning frequently. Add tomatoes, thyme and sherry and cook gently until tomatoes are soft and livers cooked through, about 3 minutes, stirring well. Cook rice in boiling, salted water, arrange in a ring on serving dish and pour chicken liver mixture in centre. Remove thyme stems and serve at once. Serves 2.

Deep-Fried Chicken Livers

A deep saucepan with a frying-basket is best for this dish, which I first tasted in New Orleans in a small restaurant near the fascinating produce market. The chicken livers were served with crisply fried onions—the onion rings dipped in batter and deep fried—absolutely delicious.

1 lb (400 g) chicken livers	flour
1 cup French dressing with garlic and herbs (page 147)	salt and pepper cooking oil
dash cayenne pepper	finely chopped parsley

Wash and trim livers, but leave whole unless they are very large. Place in a large, shallow dish and pour French dressing over them, turning to coat with the dressing. Leave for about 30 minutes, turning several times.

Heat oil slowly until a square of bread browns in 60 seconds. Drain livers and toss in a strong paper bag with the flour seasoned with salt, pepper and cayenne, until well coated all over.

Deep-fry only as many chicken livers at one time as will go in one layer in the frying-basket, frying quickly or they will be tough. Drain on kitchen paper and keep hot while all the livers are fried. Serve sprinkled with chopped parsley. Serves 4.

Chicken Liver Risotto

8 oz (200 g) chicken livers	8 oz (200 g) long grain rice
4 oz butter or margarine	2 pints (1 litre) chicken stock
2 oz mushrooms, sliced	2 tbsp sherry
1 large onion	grated Parmesan cheese
1 red *or* green pepper	salt and pepper

Wash and trim livers and cut in slices. Heat the butter in a large frying pan and turn the livers in the hot butter until stiffened. Remove with a slotted spoon and keep hot. Fry onion in the same pan until tender, then add mushrooms, diced pepper (be sure to remove seeds) and rice and stir well, cook for 5 minutes, then stir in hot stock. Cook gently until liquid has been absorbed, stirring at intervals, then add sherry, taste for seasoning and stir in chicken livers. Re-heat for 2 minutes and serve, sprinkled with Parmesan cheese. Serves 4.

Chicken Liver Vol-au-Vents

These are very good to serve for a buffet party or as the first course for a dinner party, in which case the vol-au-vent cases should be a little larger, allowing one to a serve.

8 baked 3 inch (7 cm) vol-au-vent pastry cases
1 oz (25 g) butter
1 large onion, chopped
1 clove garlic, crushed
1 lb (400 g) chicken livers
½ oz (15 g) flour
½ pint (250 ml) chicken stock
1 tbsp Worcestershire sauce
1 tbsp red wine (optional)
salt and pepper
8 parsley sprigs

Wash and trim chicken livers and cut into slices. Heat butter in a thick pan and fry onion and garlic for 5 minutes. Add liver and cook, stirring often, until stiffened and lightly browned. Stir in flour and cook for 1 minute, then stir in stock, wine if using and sauce. Bring to boil and simmer for 3 or 4 minutes, season to taste. Heat pastry cases and fill with chicken liver mixture, garnish each with a parsley sprig and serve at once. Serves 4.

Spaghetti Florentine

Florence is a charming old city, full of art and architecture, and some excellent restaurants. This is one of my favourite Florentine dishes.

12 oz (300 g) chicken livers
3 oz (75 g) butter
1 large onion, chopped
1 clove garlic, crushed
4 oz (100 g) mushrooms, sliced
14 oz (396 g) can whole, peeled tomatoes
½ cup chicken stock
2 tbsp dry white wine
½ tsp dried mixed herbs
salt and pepper
2 tbsp tomato paste
12 oz (300 g) spaghetti
grated Parmesan cheese

Wash chicken livers and halve. Heat butter in a large pan and sauté livers until lightly browned, 3 to 4 minutes. Remove from pan and keep hot. Add onion, garlic and mushrooms to pan and cook until tender. Add tomatoes and juice, tomato paste, wine, herbs, stock, salt and pepper and simmer gently, covered, for 20 minutes. Chop livers and return to pan, re-heat.

While sauce is cooking, put spaghetti into a large saucepan of boiling, salted water and cook until just tender, about 12 minutes. Drain well and serve with the sauce poured over the top, sprinkle with grated cheese. Serves 4 or 5.

Chinese Style Chicken Livers

An easily made dish for two for a special occasion, especially when accompanied by a bottle of good red wine.

8 oz (200 g) chicken livers	2 tbsp dry sherry
1 tbsp cornflour	2 tbsp cooking oil
½ tsp ground ginger	salt and pepper
1 tbsp soya sauce	cooked rice

Mix cornflour with ginger, soya sauce and sherry in a bowl and add washed, trimmed and halved chicken livers, mixing well together. Leave for half an hour. Heat oil in a frying pan, add the liver mixture and cook for 3–4 minutes over moderate heat, stirring well. Serve over hot cooked rice. Serves 2.

Sweet-Sour Chicken Livers

Another dish inspired by Chinese cooking.

1 lb (400 g) chicken livers	2 fl oz (50 ml) vinegar
3 tbsp soya sauce	salt and pepper
2 tbsp vegetable oil	1 tsp sugar
11 oz (312 g) can pineapple chunks	2 tbsp cornflour
4 oz (100 g) blanched almonds	cooked rice

Wash and trim chicken livers, and cut in halves. Place in a bowl and pour soya sauce over, leaving for a few minutes. Heat the oil in a large frying pan, add the drained chicken livers and cook for 5 minutes, turning frequently. Drain pineapple chunks and reserve the juice. Add pineapple and almonds with a slotted spoon and keep warm over boiling water.

Measure pineapple juice and if necessary make up to 1 cup with water, add vinegar, remaining soya sauce and sugar and add liquid to the pan and bring to the boil. Blend cornflour with a little water and stir into pan, cook over low heat, stirring frequently, until sauce is thick and smooth. Taste for seasoning. Replace chicken livers, pineapple and almonds and re-heat without boiling, then pour over the cooked rice. Serve at once. Serves 4.

Spiced Chicken Livers

Chicken livers are very versatile and blend happily with many different flavours. This recipe is a good example.

1 lb (400 g) chicken livers	½ tsp ground allspice
1 small onion, sliced thinly	salt and pepper
2 tbsp butter	1 tsp lemon juice
½ sweet red pepper, chopped	1 tbsp cornflour
½ pint (250 ml) chicken stock	finely chopped parsley
1 tsp brown sugar	cooked noodles

Wash and trim chicken livers and cut in halves. Sauté the onion and red pepper for 2 or 3 minutes in the butter in a large, thick pan, turning frequently, then add chicken livers and cook until stiffened. Add chicken stock, allspice, sugar, lemon juice, salt and pepper and cook slowly for 5 or 6 minutes, stirring once. Blend cornflour with a little water or chicken stock and stir into pan until boiling and thickened. Add parsley and taste for seasoning, pour over cooked noodles and toss lightly together. Serve at once. Serves 4.

Chicken Liver Pancakes

Pancakes for this dish can be made up ahead of time and stored in refrigerator with greaseproof paper between each one until just before serving time.

4 6-inch (18 cm) pancakes	2 tbsp cream
1 lb (400 g) chicken livers	2 heaped tsp flour
4 oz (100 g) mushrooms	salt and pepper
2 tbsp butter	pinch cayenne pepper
juice ½ lemon	1 tbsp grated Parmesan
pinch dried thyme	cheese

Melt 1½ tbsp butter in a thick pan. Wash and trim chicken livers and cut in quarters, add with the sliced mushrooms, thyme, lemon juice and seasonings to the pan and cook all together, stirring at intervals, for 4 minutes. Cream flour and remaining butter together and add with the cream to the mixture, cooking, covered, for 2 or 3 minutes.

Spread out the pancakes and place about 4 tbsp of liver and mushroom mixture on one side, then carefully roll up. Place in a shallow ovenproof dish, seam-side down, pour remainder of mixture over them, sprinkle with grated cheese and put into a hot oven just until lightly browned and heated through. Serves 4.

Chicken Livers Espagnole

Rice is a perfect accompaniment to chicken livers, and in this dish the liver mixture is served over well flavoured turmeric rice.

2 tbsp olive oil
1 clove garlic, chopped fine
2 stalks celery, chopped
1 medium onion, sliced
2 tbsp chopped parsley
few sprigs fresh thyme and marjoram
1 bay leaf
salt and pepper
14 oz (396 g) can tomatoes
1 small sweet red pepper
1 tsp lemon juice
4 oz (100 g) mushrooms
2 tbsp butter *or* chicken fat
1 lb (400 g) chicken livers

Heat olive oil in a fairly large saucepan and cook onion and garlic for 5 minutes then add celery, herbs and red pepper, which has been de-seeded and sliced, and cook all together until celery is tender. Mash the canned tomatoes and add with sliced mushrooms and lemon juice, salt and pepper and cook, covered, until you have a thick sauce.

Melt butter or fat in a frying pan until quite hot, but do not allow to burn, and sauté halved chicken livers for 4 or 5 minutes, until stiffened and just cooked, turning often. Add to sauce and barely simmer over very low heat for a few minutes. Serve over turmeric rice.

Turmeric Rice: This takes about 30 minutes to cook, so commence it about the same time as you start to cook the tomato sauce. Heat 2 tbsp oil in a large saucepan with a lid, then add 1 cup long-grain rice, 1 tsp salt, ¼ tsp turmeric and stir in 2 cups boiling water. Cover and simmer for 30 minutes, until rice is tender. Shake the pan at intervals, but do not stir. Serves 4.

King of Prussia's Favourite Dish

I have not been able to find out which King of Prussia so liked this dish, but it is certainly quite a simple and tasty way of cooking the chicken livers, German-style.

1 lb (400 g) chicken livers
4 oz (100 g) butter
salt and pepper
1 tbsp chopped fresh marjoram
2 lb boiled potatoes

Wash and trim chicken livers and cut in slices. Heat the butter in a thick pan and sauté the chicken livers with the marjoram until livers are stiffened and just cooked through, about 5 to 6 minutes. Immediately pour over potatoes and serve.

Chicken Livers Budapest

1 lb (400 g) chicken livers
1 oz (25 g) butter *or* bacon fat
½ tsp dried thyme *or* marjoram
1 medium onion, chopped
½ oz (15 g) flour
salt and pepper
6 oz (150 g) mushrooms
5 fl oz (150 ml) yogurt
5 fl oz (150 ml) chicken stock
½ tsp paprika

Wash and trim chicken livers and cut in halves. Melt the fat in a thick frying pan and add the herbs and paprika, then the liver halves and brown very gently. Using a slotted spoon remove liver from pan and keep hot. In the same pan fry the onion until soft then blend in the flour, salt and pepper, add sliced mushrooms and pour in the hot stock, stirring until mixture just comes to the boil. Reduce heat and add liver, and allow to simmer very gently for about 5 minutes.

Take 2 tbsp liquid from the pan and mix with the yogurt, then add yogurt to the pan, stirring gently into mixture. Reheat just until sauce is hot, but do not allow to boil. Serve with cooked rice or noodles. Serves 4.

Chicken Liver Veneziana

Liver Veneziana, made with young calf's liver, is one of the traditional dishes of Venice, but it is equally as good made with chicken livers as given here.

1 lb (400 g) chicken livers	6 large fresh sage leaves
4 medium size onions	salt and pepper
4 tbsp olive oil	4 tbsp red wine
1 tbsp chopped parsley	boiled potatoes

Wash and trim livers and cut in quarters. Slice the onions paper thin and chop sage leaves. Heat oil in a thick pan and fry onions until golden brown, turning to brown evenly. Add chicken livers and cook for 2 minutes, stirring to cook on all sides. Add parsley, sage and seasoning and the wine and cook for just long enough to dissolve the sediment in the pan, turning ingredients over several times. This is meant to be a fairly dry dish. Serve at once with plain boiled potatoes.

If sage is not available another herb can be used, but it is the sage that gives it the distinctive flavour. Serves 4.

Tyrolean Chicken Livers

Served with boiled potatoes and a green salad this dish makes a quickly cooked meal for two.

8 oz (200 g) chicken livers	1 tsp chopped capers
2 oz (50 g) butter	1 tsp grated lemon rind
1 tbsp flour	salt and pepper
4 fl oz (100 ml) sour cream	

Wash and trim livers then cut in halves. Toss in flour until well coated then fry quickly in the hot butter, turning to cook on both sides. Add cream, capers and lemon rind, stirring well together and cook for 2 or 3 minutes until heated through. Season to taste and serve at once. Serves 2.

Curried Chicken Livers

Serve these curried livers with the traditional accompaniments to curry—separate bowls of chutney, chopped egg yolks, peanuts, chopped spring onions, sliced cucumbers and raisins.

1½ lb (700 g) chicken livers	3 tsp curry powder
2 onions, sliced thinly	salt and pepper

1 clove of garlic, chopped ½ pint (250 ml) sour cream *or*
1 tbsp butter yogurt
1 tbsp oil

Wash livers, trim and cut into halves. Heat butter and oil together in a large thick pan and fry onions and garlic until onion is transparent. Stir in curry powder (amount depends on personal taste) and fry for 2 minutes. Add livers and fry for 3 minutes, turning all the time to cook evenly. Stir in sour cream or yogurt and cook over low heat just until really hot, but do not allow to boil. Serve over cooked rice. Serves 6.

Chicken Liver Tartlets
Delicious for buffet parties or as an hors d'oeuvre.

8 small pastry tartlets, baked 2 oz (50 g) mushrooms,
½ pint (250 ml) Bechamel chopped
sauce (see page 144) 2 tbsp Marsala wine *or* sweet
1 tsp chopped parsley sherry
6 oz (150 g) chicken livers

Wash, trim and slice livers and cook in the wine for 2–3 minutes until just stiffened. Add mushrooms and cook for 2 minutes with the parsley. Mix livers and mushrooms with the sauce and fill pastry tartlets. Serve hot or cold.

Chicken Liver Appetizers
Serve these as hors d'oeuvre or for a buffet party.

8 large chicken livers 4 tbsp soya sauce
24 whole water chestnuts ½ tsp curry powder
8 rashers bacon pinch ground ginger

Combine soya sauce, curry powder and ground ginger in a wide, shallow bowl. Wash and trim chicken livers and cut each one into three pieces. Cut rind from bacon, stretch each rasher with the back of a knife and cut into three pieces. Put a piece of chicken liver with a water chestnut and wrap a strip of bacon around it, fastening with a wooden toothpick. Repeat until all are used up, then place the bacon-wrapped rolls in the soya sauce mixture for about 1 hour, turning halfway through. Drain well and either grill or fry rolls, turning frequently, until bacon is crisp.

With Chicken Breasts

Chicken Breasts

Breast of chicken when removed raw from one side of the bird in a skinless, boneless piece is called a suprême, and each chicken possesses two of these. The breast of a cooked chicken in culinary French is called a blanc de poulet, or white meat of chicken.

Being tender it is easy to cook, but care must be taken that it is not overdone, or it toughens and becomes dry. Press the top of it with a finger if you think it is cooked—if it is still soft and yields slightly to the touch it is not quite done, but as soon as the flesh springs back with a gentle resilience, it is ready. Cooking time should be about 8 to 10 minutes.

You can buy chicken breasts, either fresh or frozen, prepacked from most supermarkets, or you can remove the breasts from a whole bird and cook them separately. Slip your fingers between skin and flesh and pull off the skin. Cut against the ridge of the backbone to loosen the flesh from the bone. Disjoint the wing where it joins the carcass and continue down along the rib-cage, pulling flesh from bone as you cut until the meat separates from the bone in one piece. Remove the wing, cut and pull out the white tendon that runs down the underside of the meat. Trim the edges and flatten the suprêmes lightly with the side of a heavy knife. They are now ready for cooking as in any of the following recipes. If not used, immediately wrap in greaseproof paper or film and put in refrigerator.

Suprêmes with Lemon Sauce

One of the simplest ways of cooking chicken breasts.

4 chicken breasts, boned and skinned	salt and pepper
2 tbsp butter	2 tbsp lemon juice
6 tbsp white wine *or* chicken stock	¼ pint (150 ml) cream
	lemon slices

Heat butter in a thick pan and fry chicken breasts on both sides until they are golden. Add wine or chicken stock and cook until chicken is tender about 8 minutes. Remove to heated serving dish and keep warm. Stir lemon juice into pan and stir well, then add cream and season to taste, heating without allowing to boil. Pour over chicken breasts and garnish with lemon slices. Serves 4.

Chicken Breasts au Gratin

4 boned and skinned chicken breasts
4 slices Gruyere cheese
4 slices cooked ham
1 egg, beaten lightly
brown breadcrumbs
1 tbsp flour
salt and pepper
oil *or* fat for frying

Slit the chicken breasts in halves lengthwise without cutting completely through at one end. Cut cheese slices and ham the same shape as the chicken pieces and make a 'sandwich' with the chicken filled with ham and cheese. Season flour with salt and pepper and coat filled chicken pieces in flour, then dip in beaten egg and finally in the breadcrumbs, coating well all over. Fry in hot oil or fat until crisp and golden brown on both sides, then lower heat and cook for a few more minutes. Serve with a mixed salad. Serves 4.

Suprêmes St Clair

This is another variation of the chicken, ham and cheese combination which makes a delicious dish.

4 chicken breasts
flour
salt and pepper
3 oz (75 g) butter
½ tsp dried thyme
½ pint (250 ml) chicken stock
4 oz (100 g) button mushrooms
4 slices cooked ham
4 slices Cheddar or Gruyere cheese

Skin and bone chicken breasts and coat with flour seasoned with salt, pepper and thyme. Gently fry for 2 minutes on each side in half the butter, then gradually add hot stock, or half stock and half white wine may be used. Cover and simmer until chicken is cooked, about 8 minutes.

While chicken breasts are cooking fry the sliced mushrooms in remainder of butter in a separate pan.

When breasts are cooked, remove from pan and drain well. Cut cheese and ham slices the same size as the chicken pieces, place a slice of ham on each breast, then a layer of cooked mushrooms and cover with a slice of cheese. Put under a medium griller until cheese is just melting, but do not allow to brown.

At the same time add stock from cooking chicken breasts to the pan in which mushrooms were cooked and cook for several minutes, stirring, until slightly reduced. Serve in sauce boat. Serves 4.

Chicken Kiev

This is a classic Russian dish which is rather fiddly to make, but well worth the trouble for a special dinner party.

8 chicken breasts
4 oz (100 g) butter
1 tbsp chopped parsley
1 tbsp chopped chives
1 clove garlic, crushed
salt and pepper

2 oz (50 g) flour
2 eggs, lightly beaten
6 oz (150 g) stale white breadcrumbs
oil for deep-frying

Cream the butter until soft, then beat in parsley, chives, garlic and pepper until mixed. Divide into 8 portions, and shape into small ovals. Chill well—they should be very hard.

Skin and bone chicken breasts, place between 2 sheets of thick greaseproof paper and pound thin, being careful not to break the pieces. Remove from paper and place one portion of the chilled butter on each chicken breast, folding the chicken meat around the butter, envelope-fashion, so that the butter is completely enclosed and sealed in. Tie each little parcel with white thread to hold in place if necessary.

Dip each chicken parcel first in flour, coating well, then into the beaten eggs and lastly into the breadcrumbs, pressing crumbs in firmly to make a good layer all over.

Put prepared chicken breasts into refrigerator for an hour before frying.

Have oven pre-heated to cool (250°F, 130°C or No. $\frac{1}{2}$) to keep chicken parcels warm as they are fried. Heat oil in a deep frying saucepan with a basket, and test if it is hot enough by frying a cube of stale bread, which should turn golden in 1 minute. Fry the prepared breasts two at a time for about 5 or 6 minutes each until golden brown. As each batch is fried drain on kitchen paper and place on a serving dish in oven to keep warm. Do all this as quickly as possible until all chicken parcels have been fried, then serve at once with creamy mashed potatoes and a green vegetable such as peas.

If preferred, plain butter can be used for the filling. Serves 6–8.

Chicken Suprêmes Missouri

This is a recipe I collected from my hostess on a visit to Missouri, and it makes a very tasty meal served on rice.

6 chicken breasts	2 tbsp lemon juice
1 cup sour cream	1 tsp Worcestershire sauce
1 clove garlic, crushed	soft white breadcrumbs
salt, pepper, paprika	3 oz (75 g) butter
chicken stock *or* white wine	

Mix sour cream, garlic, lemon juice, Worcestershire sauce, salt, pepper and paprika together and pour over chicken breasts in an ovenproof dish. Leave for several hours.

When ready to cook sprinkle thickly with breadcrumbs and place a generous pat of butter on top of each chicken breast. Bake in a moderate oven (350°F, 180°C or No. 4) for 10 to 15 minutes until chicken feels springy when cooked. If necessary, add a little chicken stock or white wine to the side of the dish, not over it, to prevent cooking dry. Serve with lemon quarters to be squeezed over the top after serving. Serves 6.

Suprêmes Soave

This gets its name from the delicious Italian white wine in which it is cooked.

4 chicken breasts	4 oz (100 g) button mushrooms
4 tbsp butter	
½ cup Soave wine	2 tbsp butter (extra)
2 tbsp chopped onion	2 tbsp chicken stock
salt and pepper	½ pint (250 ml) soured cream
	1 tbsp chopped parsley

Melt 4 tbsp butter in thick pan and brown the skinned and boned chicken breasts, turning several times to brown evenly. Pour 1 cup wine over chicken, cover and steam until tender, about 8 minutes, shaking pan at intervals. While chicken is cooking melt extra butter in another pan and fry onion and sliced mushrooms until tender, stir in stock and soured cream. Remove from heat. When chicken is tender pour sour cream sauce over it, season to taste and re-heat but do not allow to boil. Sprinkle with the chopped parsley to serve. Serves 4.

Chicken Chianti

In this recipe the chicken breasts are cooked in the famous Italian Chianti red wine for a change of flavour. This is a dish I tasted in Siena, in the heart of the Chianti wine producing region, one of the loveliest parts of Tuscany.

4 chicken breasts	2 tbsp tomato paste
salt and pepper	1 tbsp chopped onion
3 oz (75 g) butter	½ cup Chianti
1 tbsp olive oil	2 tbsp chopped parsley

Flatten the chicken breasts slightly. Sprinkle with salt and pepper and leave for a minute while you heat the butter and oil together in a thick frying pan. Add the chicken pieces and cook for 3 minutes, turning to lightly brown both sides. Remove from pan and keep hot.

Lightly brown the onion in the same pan, blend in the tomato paste, chopped parsley and wine and replace the chicken breasts in the pan. Cover and simmer gently until chicken is springy to the touch, about 8 to 10 minutes. Remove from pan and quickly boil up the liquor in the pan until slightly reduced. Pour over chicken breasts and serve at once. Drink more Chianti with the dish. Serves 4.

Chicken Breasts Piquant

4 chicken breasts	1 tsp ground ginger
2 tbsp soya sauce	1 tsp brown sugar
2 tbsp oil	¼ pint (150 ml) dry cider
1 crushed clove garlic	boiled rice
6 tbsp chicken stock	chopped parsley

Mix together soya sauce, oil, cider, garlic, ginger, brown sugar and chicken stock, pour over chicken breasts in ovenproof dish and stand for an hour. Place in a moderate oven (375°F, 190°C or No. 5), covered, and cook for 10 to 15 minutes, or until springy when chicken is tested.

Arrange chicken breasts on a bed of rice and pour sauce from baking dish over, then sprinkle with parsley. Serves 4.

Suprêmes à la Marsala

Marsala is a sweet dessert wine produced in Sicily, but this recipe can be made with either port or Madeira if preferred.

4 chicken breasts	2 oz (50 g) fine white bread-
salt and pepper	crumbs
4 oz (100 g) flour	1 tbsp chopped shallots *or*
1 egg beaten with	spring onions
½ tsp olive oil	¼ pint (150 ml) chicken stock
2 oz (50 g) grated Parmesan	2 tbsp Marsala wine
cheese	2 tbsp chopped parsley
2 oz (50 g) butter	

Season the suprêmes with salt and pepper and roll them in flour. Dip in the beaten egg and oil then roll in the cheese and breadcrumbs mixed together, pressing the crumbs well in to make a thick coating all over. Leave to set for at least an hour.

Heat the butter in a thick pan and sauté the chicken on both sides for 6 to 8 minutes until it feels springy when pressed with a finger. Keep hot while you make the sauce.

After removing suprêmes from the pan stir in the shallots or spring onions and fry until tender. Pour in the wine and chicken stock mixing well with contents of pan and boil rapidly until slightly thickened and syrupy. Pour over suprêmes, sprinkle with parsley and serve at once.

For a change either 4 oz (100 g) sliced button mushrooms or half a sweet red pepper, sliced, can be added to the sauce, frying with the shallots. It may be necessary to add a little extra butter to the pan. Serves 4.

Suprêmes Garibaldi

4 chicken breasts, skinned	6 large mushrooms, sliced
3 eggs, beaten lightly	6 slices Gruyere cheese
1 cup fine breadcrumbs	½ cup chicken stock
3 oz (75 g) butter *or* margarine	juice ½ lemon

Cut each chicken breast in halves, lengthwise and leave in beaten eggs for 1 hour. Drain and roll in breadcrumbs, coating well. Heat butter in a flameproof casserole and fry chicken slices on both sides until golden, about 2 minutes. Cover with the mushrooms and cover mushrooms with cheese slices. Add stock.

Put casserole into a moderate oven (350°F, 180°C or No. 4) and cook for about 30 minutes, Uncover, squeeze lemon juice over the top and serve at once. Serves 4.

Suprêmes with Hazelnuts

2 chicken breasts, skinned
flour
salt and pepper
1 egg yolk
1 tbsp oil
fresh white breadcrumbs
1 tbsp butter
10 fl oz (250 ml) chicken stock
2 heaped tsp cornflour
3 fl oz (75 ml) cream
1 oz shelled hazelnuts
1 tsp lemon juice
1 fl oz (25 ml) brandy *or* sherry

Put hazelnuts through the fine blade of a mincer. Toss chicken breasts in seasoned flour, then brush over with the egg lightly beaten with 2 tsp oil and lastly dip in breadcrumbs until well coated, pressing the crumbs into the chicken.

Melt butter and remainder of oil in a thick pan and gently fry chicken breasts until golden brown on both sides, put aside and keep hot while you make the sauce. Mix cornflour with a little of the chicken stock, put remainder of stock in the pan and boil hard for a few minutes, then stir in blended cornflour until thickened. Slowly add cream, then minced nuts and brandy or sherry, stirring well. Season to taste with salt, pepper and lemon juice and pour over chicken breasts. Serves 2.

Suprêmes in Foil

Serve these tasty parcels in the foil in which they cook.

2 large chicken breasts
2 oz (50 g) butter
1 tbsp chopped onion
2 tbsp diced carrot
2 oz (50 g) button mushrooms
salt and pepper
1 tbsp finely chopped celery
2 slices Gruyere cheese
2 slices cooked ham, cut fairly thick
4 oz (100 g) tomatoes, peeled
cooking foil

Beat chicken breasts until fairly thin. Heat butter in a thick pan and sauté chicken breasts for one minute each side. Remove from pan and gently fry the onions, celery and carrots turning to cook evenly. Add sliced mushrooms and cook for 2 minutes.

Place one ham slice on a square of foil which has been well buttered, then place chicken breast on top, then a slice of cheese, half the chopped and seeded tomatoes and lastly half the vegetable mixture. Season with salt and pepper and fold the foil firmly on top and at each end to make a good parcel. Repeat with remainder of ingredients in the same way. Bake in a hot oven (450°F, 230°C or No. 8) for 10 minutes. Serves 2.

Chicken and Ham Rolls

Serve these rolls on a bed of plain boiled rice which has been tossed with finely chopped parsley.

4 chicken breasts, skinned	1 small onion, chopped fine
½ lb (200 g) mushrooms	1 clove garlic
butter *or* chicken fat	8 slices cooked ham
salt, pepper, nutmeg	3 tbsp sweet sherry

Heat butter or chicken fat in a thick pan and fry the onion and the whole clove of garlic until soft and golden brown. Remove garlic and discard. Flatten chicken breasts slightly and cut in halves lengthwise. Sauté in the same pan, adding more butter if necessary, for 3 or 4 minutes until cooked on both sides, then remove and keep hot. Add sliced mushrooms to pan and fry for 5 minutes over fairly high heat, turning at intervals. Season with salt, pepper and a little ground nutmeg.

Have the ham cut thin enough to roll but not so thin that it will break when rolled. Place half a chicken breast on each slice of ham, then some mushrooms and roll up the ham. Tie with thread and place in a buttered ovenproof dish. Repeat this procedure with remainder of ingredients, dividing the mushrooms between the slices as evenly as possible. Put all the rolls in the dish, seam side downwards, pour sherry over the top and put into a medium oven (350°F, 180°C or No. 4) for just long enough to heat rolls through. Serve at once. Serves 4.

Sauces and Stuffings

Sauces and Stuffings

A plain boiled fowl can be given new flavours and added interest with a good sauce, one usually made with the strained stock from cooking the bird. If this stock is not available use chicken-stock cubes, but be careful when adding seasoning to the sauce as the cubes are already salted.

Bread Sauce

This is a traditional English accompaniment to chicken, and can be made with half milk and half chicken stock if preferred.

½ pint (250 ml) milk
1 medium onion
2 whole cloves
small bay leaf

3 or 4 tbsp fresh white breadcrumbs
salt and white pepper
½ oz (15 g) butter

Stick cloves into peeled onion and put into saucepan with milk and bay leaf, bring to boil then remove from stove, cover and leave to infuse for 15 minutes.

Remove onion and bay leaf from milk and add breadcrumbs, simmer over low heat for about 5 minutes until thick and creamy, season to taste and stir in butter until melted. Serve at once.

Béchamel Sauce

This is a good basic sauce, to which can be added either capers, chopped cooked asparagus, chopped cooked mushrooms, prepared horseradish or sliced stuffed olives, any of which are good over steamed or fried chicken.

1 oz (25 g) lean bacon, diced
2 oz (50 g) chopped onion
1 oz (25 g) butter
½ oz (15 g) flour

¼ pint (150 ml) chicken stock
¼ pint (150 ml) cream
salt and pepper to taste

Melt butter in a thick pan and fry bacon and onion for 4–5 minutes, turning often. Stir in flour and cook for a few minutes, then gradually stir in stock and cream, stirring well until thickened. Simmer for 5 minutes, then strain. Serve hot.

Brown Mushroom Sauce

½ lb (200 g) small mushrooms
2 tbsp butter *or* margarine
1 clove of garlic, crushed
1 pint (500 ml) chicken stock
2 tbsp plain flour
salt and pepper to taste

Wash mushrooms and slice. Melt butter in pan and cook garlic for a few minutes until golden, then discard. Add mushrooms and cook for 5 minutes, turning frequently. Stir in flour and brown lightly, then stir in chicken stock and continue stirring until thickened. Taste for seasoning, cover and simmer 5 minutes, stirring occasionally. If a thinner sauce is required add a little more stock.

Mixed Herb Sauce

½ oz (15g) butter *or* margarine
½ oz (15 g) plain flour
¼ pint (150 ml) sour cream
¼ pint (150 ml) chicken stock
1 tsp chopped chives
1 tsp chopped basil
1 tsp chopped sage
1 tsp chopped parsley

Melt butter and blend in flour, cook for 2 minutes then stir in chicken stock and cream, stirring until smooth and thickened. Remove from heat and quickly beat in chopped herbs. Re-heat.

Paprika Sauce from Hungary

2 oz (50 g) butter *or* margarine
1 oz (25 g) plain flour
2 tbsp finely chopped onion
¼ pint white wine
2 tsp paprika
¾ pint (400 ml) chicken stock

Melt half the butter in saucepan and stir in flour, cook for 2 minutes then stir in stock and continue stirring until smooth and thickened, then cook gently for 5 minutes, stirring at intervals. While it is cooking melt remainder of butter in a small pan and fry onion until transparent, but do not allow to brown. Add wine and simmer until reduced by half. Add this to first sauce and stir in paprika, season to taste and simmer for 5 minutes.

This sauce should be rose coloured and well flavoured, and more paprika may be added if desired, or a little tomato paste can be added to the sauce for the last cooking.

Make sure the paprika used is fresh and a good red colour, as stale paprika tastes musty and would spoil the sauce and the flavour of the chicken.

Quick Hollandaise Sauce

This is a quick and easy version of a classic sauce made in an electric blender. Serve it over poached or sautéed chicken breasts garnished with asparagus.

3 egg yolks	dash cayenne pepper
1 tbsp lemon juice	4 oz (100 g) butter

Melt the butter, and while it is melting place egg yolks, cayenne and lemon juice in blender container, cover and just turn blender on and then off. With blender turned to high speed slowly pour in melted butter, blending until mixture is light and fluffy, about 30 seconds.

Place sauce over warm, not hot, water until ready to serve.

Tomato Sauce

A sauce with many uses, as it can be served over chicken pieces, over chicken livers or for a change as the sauce over roast chicken in place of the usual gravy.

1 tbsp olive oil	salt and pepper
1½ lbs (700 g) ripe tomatoes	1 tsp tomato paste
1 medium onion, sliced	2 tsp Worcestershire sauce
1 stalk celery, chopped	½ oz (15 g) butter *or* margarine
bouquet garni	1 tbsp flour

Heat oil in a thick saucepan and cook onion and celery until soft. Add ripe tomatoes, sliced, bouquet garni, tomato paste, sauce, salt and pepper and simmer, covered for 30 minutes. Press mixture through a sieve, first removing bouquet garni. Do not use a blender for this as it does not remove the seeds.

In a clean saucepan melt the butter, stir in the flour and cook for 1 minute, then stir in tomato sauce and stir until it boils and thickens.

The last part may be omitted if a thin sauce is required.

Blended Curry Sauce

½ pint (250 ml) milk	2 tsp lemon juice
1 oz (25 g) butter *or* **margarine**	2 tsp tomato paste
1 oz (25 g) flour	1 tbsp chutney
3 *or* 4 tsp curry powder	salt and pepper

Heat milk with butter or margarine until melted. Pour into electric blender with remainder of ingredients and blend until smooth. Pour into saucepan and stir continuously until sauce boils and thickens, simmer for 2 minutes.

Piquant Sauce
Good over grilled chicken legs

½ oz (15 g) butter
1 small onion, chopped small
1 tsp tomato paste
2 tsp Worcestershire sauce
½ tsp prepared mustard
½ pint (250 ml) chicken stock
1 bay leaf

Melt butter in pan and fry onion for 5 minutes. Add remaining ingredients and bring to the boil, then boil gently for 10 minutes, uncovered. Remove bay leaf before serving.

Indonesian Sauce
This makes a good basting sauce for grilled or barbecued chicken.

1 tbsp cooking oil
4 tbsp peanut butter
¼ cup tomato ketchup
3 tbsp Worcestershire sauce
1 clove garlic, crushed
salt and pepper

Heat oil gently in a small pan with garlic, when hot add peanut butter and stir over low heat until peanut butter begins to darken and thicken slightly. Remove from heat at once and stir in ketchup and sauce, salt and pepper. Remove garlic and leave for at least 2 hours before using. If sauce is too thick, add a little water or chicken stock and re-heat gently.

French Dressing
This is the classic French dressing used for salads, sometimes called Sauce Vinaigrette. A simple way of making this is to put all ingredients into a bottle with a tight stopper and shake well. It will keep for a week, and should be well shaken before using. Olive oil makes the best dressing, but any good salad oil can be used.

2 tbsp wine vinegar
salt and pepper
6 tbsp olive oil
pinch dry mustard

If preferred, half vinegar and half lemon juice can be used, and many people like to add ½ tsp sugar.

For those who do not like too much oil I use equal amounts of salad oil and vinegar, with 1 tsp lemon juice and a pinch each of sugar and mustard, with salt and pepper. If using the dressing at once, fresh herbs such as finely chopped tarragon, parsley or chives can be added, with a crushed clove of garlic, and well shaken before using.

Mayonnaise

Most salads benefit from a good mayonnaise, and although there are some very good bottled mayonnaises available it is always better to make your own. This is much easier if you have an electric blender (liquidiser) which makes the job very simple.

Mayonnaise is easier to make when all ingredients are at normal room temperature. Remove eggs from refrigerator some time before using, and rinse the container of the blender out with warm water, but be sure it is completely dry before adding the egg. Wine vinegar, if obtainable, is preferable to the stronger malt vinegar, and the traditional recipe calls for olive oil, but any good salad oil can be used.

1 whole egg	1 tbsp vinegar
½ tsp dry mustard	½ pint (250 ml) oil
½ tsp salt	

Break egg into the blender container, add mustard and salt. Cover and blend for 30 seconds until thick and foamy, add vinegar and blend for 10 seconds. Uncover container and while blending at high speed pour oil into the centre of the egg mixture in a very slow stream, almost by drops. The sauce will begin to thicken after about half the oil has been added, but continue adding oil until too thick to whirl in the blender. Scrape into a bowl or wide-mouthed jar and taste for seasoning, stirring in more if necessary.

This will keep for up to a week in the refrigerator if kept well covered, and gives about ¾ pint (400 ml) mayonnaise.

Mayonnaise Verte

This mayonnaise to which green herbs have been added makes an excellent sauce with cold boiled chicken and salad.

¾ pint (400 ml) mayonnaise
8–10 young spinach leaves
2 tbsp chopped shallots *or* spring onions
1 oz (25 g) watercress leaves
4 tbsp parsley heads
1 tbsp fresh tarragon leaves *or* ½ tbsp dried tarragon

Add spinach leaves and shallots or onions to ½ pint (250 ml) boiling water and boil for 2 minutes. Add remainder of herbs and boil 1 minute more. Strain, run cold water over them and pat dry with a cloth. Put through blender and add to mayonnaise, or if making mayonnaise from the beginning, add herbs to the egg in blender and proceed as given in recipe above.

Coating Mayonnaise

An ideal mayonnaise for coating cold, boiled or poached chicken is this one in which gelatine is dissolved. A dish of chicken breasts or drumsticks coated with this and well chilled and decorated with strips of red and green peppers and hard boiled egg yolks looks very special for an important summer dinner party.

¾ pint (400 ml) mayonnaise
2 tbsp white wine
1 tbsp wine vinegar
2½ tbsp strained chicken stock
½ oz (15 g) gelatine

Pour the liquids into a small saucepan and sprinkle gelatine over it, allowing it to dissolve for several minutes. Put over low heat and stir until gelatine is completely dissolved. Cool. Beat cooled gelatine mixture into mayonnaise very gradually, the sauce will thin out, then gradually thicken as the gelatine sets. It should be used for coating chicken just before it sets, if it becomes too stiff it can be stirred over gentle heat for just a few seconds.

Mayonnaise Variations

A simple chicken salad can be made to taste quite different if various flavours are added to the mayonnaise which is served with the salad.

To one cup mayonnaise add 1 tsp curry powder and 2 tsp dessicated coconut which has been soaked in orange juice for 15 minutes. Add orange juice with the coconut.

Sauce Andalouse is made by adding 2 tbsp tomato paste, 1 tsp Worcestershire sauce and a few chopped stuffed olives to 1 cup mayonnaise.

Tartare sauce is usually served with fish, but it is also very good served over cold, boiled chicken. Add 2 tsp chopped capers, 2 tsp chopped gherkins, 1 tsp onion juice and 1 tsp lemon juice to 1 cup mayonnaise. To obtain the onion juice scrape a halved onion with a sharp-pointed spoon until you have the amount required.

When preparing these variations always allow the completed mixtures to stand for at least 30 minutes before serving to enable flavour to blend with the mayonnaise.

Cold Curry Sauce

Serve this over chicken salad instead of mayonnaise. It needs to be made at least 30 minutes before serving.

1 cup sour cream *or* yogurt	1 tsp curry powder (*or* to taste)
1 tsp prepared horseradish	½ tsp grated lemon rind
½ tsp prepared mustard	1 tbsp lemon juice
1 clove garlic, crushed	salt and pepper to taste

Beat all ingredients well together and stand in a cool place until ready to serve. Remove garlic before adding to chicken. For added colour sprinkle with chopped chives or paprika.

Marinades for Chicken

Chicken pieces can be marinaded before grilling for extra flavour, or when they are to be barbecued. Prepare the marinade at least an hour before using.

Wine and Herb Marinade:

½ pint (250 ml) dry white wine	1 tsp dried tarragon *or* thyme
3 tbsp lemon juice	2 tbsp salad oil
1 clove of garlic, crushed	salt and pepper to taste

Combine all ingredients in a saucepan and heat until just simmering – do not boil. Remove from heat, cover and stand for an hour, then pour over chicken pieces and leave for 1 to 3 hours, depending on how strong you want the marinade to flavour the chicken. Use marinade to baste the chicken as it grills.

Honey-orange Marinade:

6 tbsp clear honey	1 tsp dry mustard

½ pint (250 ml) orange juice
¼ pint (150 ml) dry white wine
1 tbsp soy sauce
1 clove of garlic, crushed

1 tsp dried mixed herbs
2 tbsp salad oil
1 tsp Worcestershire sauce
or a dash of Tabasco

Combine all ingredients and stand for about an hour, then pour over chicken and leave for 1 to 3 hours, turning once during that time. Use marinade to baste chicken as it grills.

For a Basting Sauce for a whole chicken cooked on a spit-grill combine ½ cup each of clear honey, lemon juice and melted butter, seasoned with pepper and a little mustard.

Stuffings

A savoury stuffing can make all the difference to the flavour of a roast chicken – and also helps it to go further as the stuffing is served with the chicken meat.

These days when prepared stuffing mixes are so easy to use the housewife is inclined to forget the many other ways of adding good taste to the familiar roast chicken, but the recipes given here may inspire her to try something different for a change of flavour.

Rice and Raisin

1 cup cooked rice
½ cup seedless raisins
1 tbsp butter *or* margarine
½ cup finely chopped celery

1 tbsp chopped parsley
1 tsp fresh mixed herbs, chopped
or ½ tsp dried mixed herbs
salt and pepper to taste

Cover raisins with boiling water and stand for 5 minutes, drain and dry. Drain rice well and spread out on a plate to dry. Melt butter in pan and fry celery for 5 minutes, turning frequently, add remainder of ingredients and cook for a few minutes. Leave to get cold, then stuff bird with this mixture.

If preferred, chopped mushrooms may be substituted for the raisins. They should be fried with the celery.

Ham and Olives

3 oz (75 g) stuffed green olives
3 oz (75 g) stale white bread

1 egg, lightly beaten
1 tbsp chopped parsley

4 oz (100 g) cooked ham, chopped
3 tbsp milk
½ tsp made mustard
salt and pepper to taste

Cut olives in halves. Soak cubed bread in milk and squeeze dry. Mix all ingredients together and stuff bird.

Liver and Mushroom

3 oz (75 g) mushrooms, chopped
1 chicken liver
1 tbsp butter *or* bacon fat
1 clove of garlic, crushed
1 tbsp chopped parsley
1 cup soft white breadcrumbs
1 egg yolk, lightly beaten
salt and pepper to taste

Chop liver and brown with the mushrooms in hot fat. If using garlic, brown with mushrooms then discard. Add breadcrumbs and parsley and turn in fat for a few minutes. Cool, then add egg yolk and seasonings and pack loosely into bird.

Sausage and Garlic

1 tbsp butter *or* bacon fat
1 chopped onion
1 clove garlic, crushed
½ lb (200 g) sausage meat
grated rind ½ lemon
salt and pepper

Melt fat and fry onion lightly without colouring. Fry garlic at the same time, then discard, unless you prefer a strong flavour of garlic when it can be left in the stuffing. Put sausage meat, lemon rind and seasoning in a basin, add onion and mix well together. Pack loosely into bird.

Orange and Herbs

1 oz (25 g) butter or margarine
4–5 tbsp fresh white breadcrumbs
2 tbsp chopped mixed fresh herbs
salt and pepper
2 tbsp chopped onion
grated rind and juice of an orange
1 egg lightly beaten

Melt fat and fry onion lightly with the herbs. Put breadcrumbs into basin, add onions and herbs and all other ingredients, and mix well.

Nutty-Herb with Wine

2 oz (50 g) walnuts, finely chopped
1½ cup breadcrumbs
½ tsp dried mixed herbs
1 egg, lightly beaten
salt and pepper to taste
little Madeira or sweet red wine

Mix all ingredients together, adding just enough wine (or milk if preferred) to make a good consistency. Hazelnuts or Brazilnuts may be used instead of walnuts.

Anchovy and Lemon

This comes from Poland, and is especially good for an older bird because of its strong flavour.

8–10 canned anchovies, finely chopped
1½ cup soft breadcrumbs
1 egg, lightly beaten
2 tsp lemon juice
1 tsp grated lemon rind
pepper to taste

Drain the anchovies well (use the oil to make an unusual and tasty salad dressing), and mix with other ingredients. Leave to stand for about half an hour for flavours to blend, then stuff bird loosely.

Mushroom and Onion

2 tbsp butter
1 small onion, chopped
4 oz (100 g) mushrooms, chopped
2 tbsp chicken stock
½ cup soft breadcrumbs
salt and pepper
1 small egg, beaten
2 tsp chopped parsley

Heat butter in a pan and fry onion and mushrooms until soft, turning frequently. Add stock and cook for 3 minutes. Remove from heat and add breadcrumbs, salt and pepper and mix well. Cool and fold in the beaten egg and parsley. Use at once to loosely stuff chicken.

Ham and Rice

½ cup cooked rice
1 small onion, chopped
3 oz (75 g) cooked ham
1 tbsp chopped parsley

2 tbsp butter or margarine   1 small egg
salt and pepper   1 tsp mixed mustard

The rice for this should be quite dry, preferably cooked some time before using and spread out to dry. Heat butter and fry the onion until soft, then mix in the rice and turn lightly until golden. Remove from heat and add finely chopped ham, parsley and seasonings. Leave until cool, then fold in lightly beaten egg mixing all well together. Fill chicken loosely with the mixture.

Bacon and Parsnips

This is a rather unusual stuffing, but the parsnips go very well with the chicken. I like to cook peeled and halved parsnips around the meat with potatoes, turning them to brown evenly.

8 oz (200 g) parsnips   4 oz (100 g) bacon, chopped
1 tbsp butter *or* margarine   2 tsp chopped fresh sage
1 small onion, chopped   salt and pepper

Peel parsnips, cut each in 4 lengthwise and, if necessary, cut out the hard centre core. Boil in salted water until tender, then mash them with half the butter until smooth and creamy. Heat remainder of butter in a small pan and fry the onion and bacon for a few minutes. Remove from heat and add parsnips, sage and season to taste. Stuff chicken with this mixture when it is cold.

Parsley and Celery

Use some of the young leaves of the celery in addition to the the stalk for this stuffing.

1 rasher streaky bacon   1 tbsp chopped parsley
1 oz (25 g) butter *or* margarine   ½ tsp grated lemon rind
4 oz (100 g) celery, chopped   1 egg, beaten
4 oz (100 g) soft white breadcrumbs   salt and pepper

Chop the bacon and cook for 4 or 5 minutes with the celery in butter, turning frequently. Add the breadcrumbs, parsley salt and pepper, mix well and allow to cool. Then add lemon rind and lastly the egg to bind the mixture together. Stuff chicken loosely with the mixture.

Some chopped fresh thyme or tarragon can be added to this mixture if desired.

Carrot and Orange

1 oz (25 g) butter or margarine
1 small onion, chopped
4 oz (100 g) soft breadcrumbs
6 oz (150 g) carrots, grated
grated rind and juice of ½ orange

Heat butter and cook onion and carrots until soft. Remove from pan and add breadcrumbs, orange rind and juice, mixing well together. Season with salt and pepper to taste and stuff bird. The chicken can be basted with orange juice as it cooks.

Cooking on Skewers

Cooking on Skewers

Cooking on skewers is one of the oldest known forms of cookery, and early man probably used sharpened sticks to hold bits of meat over a fire to cook, just as we do today.

The records of many countries show directions for skewer cooking under a number of different names, but the basic idea is the same, and all are delicious eating.

In Russia it is known as 'shashlik', in South Africa the housewife makes 'sosaties', while meat and vegetables cooked on skewers is called 'shish kebab' in the Near Eastern kitchens. In Malaysia and Singapore you eat 'satay' and you will find these skewered tit-bits being cooked over charcoal braziers on street corners for anyone to buy and eat on the spot.

The Japanese are very partial to small pieces of meat, chicken or fish cooked on bamboo skewers over an 'hibachi' or charcoal grill on the table, and in some of the expensive Caucasian restaurants in Paris and New York you can have your kebabs brought to your table on a steel sword instead of an ordinary skewer, and usually flamed with cognac to make it more spectacular.

The French call it 'en brochette' and one of my favourite dishes is chicken livers en brochette, which is simply halved chicken livers alternated with squares of fatty bacon on skewers, then grilled under medium heat for about 10 to 15 minutes, turning frequently as they grill, and basting with butter. These should be served on a bed of parsleyed rice.

Chicken adapts itself very well to this type of cooking as it cooks fairly quickly, the breast meat, the meat from the top of the thigh and the chicken livers being the best for this.

If you have an electric spit-grill attachment to your cooker, with skewers which rotate automatically, the task of cooking kebabs is much simpler, but they will grill very well under an ordinary gas or electric griller if care is taken to turn them frequently, basting well to prevent drying out.

Most foods, and chicken in particular because it has very little fat of its own, benefit from being marinaded for at least an hour before grilling, and usually the marinade can be used as a basting sauce.

When using oil in a marinade I find corn oil is preferable, as it gives no flavour of its own to the chicken.

There are many different kinds of skewers, but care should be taken when choosing any of the fancy ones sold in sets in souvenir shops abroad, as few of these are stainless or rustproof, and can give a nasty taste to the marinade. I prefer the stainless steel ones, myself.

When combining ingredients such as tomatoes, mushrooms, onions, bananas, red or green peppers, cubes of pineapple or squares of bacon with chicken it is important that they should be selected so that they all require the same cooking time. A kebab should be served well-cooked, not burnt, but juicy and tender, and in a number of combinations the chicken will benefit from being half-cooked before threading on skewers, particularly if thigh meat is used. The chicken can either be poached or grilled beforehand, then marinaded and allied with other ingredients on skewers for the final cooking.

Any of these kebabs would be ideal for barbecue cooking.

Chicken Kebabs

An assortment of marinades suitable for chicken will be found on page 159.

Marinate squares of chicken in pineapple marinade for an hour then thread chicken, pineapple cubes and squares of sweet red pepper alternately on skewers. Baste frequently with marinade during grilling time.

Marinate squares of chicken and 2-inch (5 cm) pieces of peeled bananas in Javanese marinade for at least an hour, then drain and wrap banana pieces in strips of bacon and thread alternately with chicken on skewers. Baste frequently while grilling.

Alternate cubes of cooked chicken, halved chicken livers and squares of bacon on skewers and dip in wine marinade for a few minutes before grilling, and baste well with marinade during grilling.

Half cook small pickling onions and chicken meat. Cut chicken into cubes and marinate with the onions and some button mushrooms for at least an hour. Thread alternate chicken, onion, mushroom and squares of sweet red pepper, with pieces of bacon between each ingredient on the skewers. Baste well while grilling.

Lemon Marinade:
1 cup lemon juice
¾ cup corn oil
1 medium onion, chopped
½ clove garlic, crushed
½ tsp dried thyme
small bay leaf, crumbled

Wine Marinade:
¾ cup dry white wine
¼ cup lemon juice
¾ cup oil
2 tbsp soya sauce

Javanese Marinade:
½ cup peanut oil
3 tbsp soya sauce
1 tbsp chopped onion
2 tsp curry powder
pinch cumin
½ tsp ground ginger

Pineapple Marinade:
1 cup pineapple juice
1 tbsp lemon juice
½ cup corn oil
2 tbsp soya sauce
few sprigs fresh thyme
clove garlic, crushed

Herb Marinade:
¼ cup dry sherry
½ cup corn oil
freshly ground pepper
1 tbsp chopped fresh mixed herbs
1 tsp lemon juice

California Marinade:
1 small onion, chopped
1 clove garlic, chopped
½ cup tomato ketchup
2 tbsp vinegar
½ cup corn oil
2 tsp Worcestershire sauce
dash of cayenne pepper
2 tsp chopped parsley

Butter Baste:
3 oz (75 g) butter, melted
1 clove garlic, crushed
3 tsp lemon juice
1 tsp chopped parsley

Heat all ingredients together, then remove garlic and use for basting any grilled chicken.

Allow 1 filled skewer for each serve, and serve on a bed of cooked rice tossed with finely chopped parsley.

(More recipes for marinades suitable for kebabs can be found on page 150).

Whole Chicken Kebab

A Pakistani method of grilling small chickens on a rotating spit over charcoal, and ideal if you have an automatic spit-grill or rotisserie attachment to your cooker. This is also good for a barbecue meal, when the amounts can be doubled.

2 to 2½ lb (900 to 1·1 kg) chicken
4 medium onions
3 cloves garlic
3 cardamom seeds
salt
chilli powder to taste
3 oz (75 g) butter

A Pakistani housewife would probably use a mortar and pestle to make this paste, but an electric blender will do the job much more quickly. Put onions, garlic, cardamom seeds, chilli powder and salt into blender container with 1 tbsp water and blend for half a minute. Rub this mixture well into the trussed chicken and leave for 30 minutes.

When ready to cook, melt butter and brush over chicken. Insert the long skewer from your rotisserie through the centre of the chicken, making sure it is firmly held. Grill under very moderate heat until chicken is tender, turning by hand if necessary, and basting with butter at intervals.

(Cardamom seeds and chilli powder can be obtained from any Indian grocery store.) Serves 2 or 3.

Skewered Poussins

Poussins or baby chickens weighing about 1½ lb (700 g) each can be grilled on skewers quite successfully, but they must be well basted as they cook or they will be dry. Any of the marinades given in preceding pages could be used. Be sure the chickens have plump breasts and legs.

Cut each chicken through the backbone but not through the breast, open it out so that it lies flat and put into chosen marinade for at least 30 minutes, turning once. Thread on long skewer of rotisserie, brush over with melted butter and grill until tender and golden brown, turning frequently and basting frequently with the marinade. Do not overcook. Serves 2 or 3.

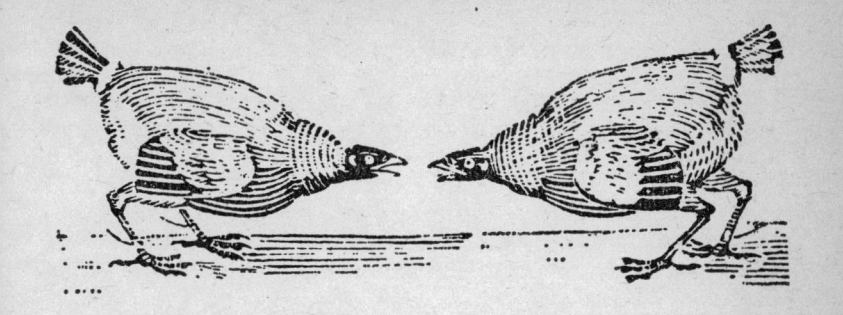

Leftovers

Leftovers

There are frequently times when only half a chicken has been used for a meal and you would prefer to serve it as another hot meal next day rather than cold with salad. Chicken leftovers can be used to make a varied assortment of tasty dishes, some of them given here, and these recipes are also worth cooking chicken pieces especially to make them up when there are no leftovers.

Greek Pilaff

Copy the Greek housewife and make good use of chicken leftovers like this.

8 oz (200 g) cooked chicken
8 oz (200 g) long grain rice
1 medium onion, chopped
2 oz (50 g) butter *or* chicken fat
2 pints (1 litre) chicken stock
2 oz (50 g) chopped walnuts
2 large tomatoes, peeled
½ tsp chopped fresh thyme
salt and pepper to taste

Using a large pan with a lid, fry onion in fat until tender. Cut chicken meat into strips and turn in the same pan, then add rice and fry gently, stirring frequently with a fork for 5 minutes. Add hot stock, chopped tomatoes, walnuts, thyme and seasoning. Cover and simmer gently until rice is tender and stock has been absorbed, stirring occasionally with a fork.

If preferred, peas may be added in place of tomatoes.

Chicken Verona

This is a rich and well-flavoured dish from Romeo and Juliet's city of Verona, in northern Italy.

2 oz (50 g) Bel Paese cheese
4 oz (100 g) cream cheese
½ pint (250 ml) thin cream
2 oz (50 g) butter
6 oz (150 g) white meat of chicken
4 oz (100 g) mushrooms, chopped
sprinkle of pepper
grated Parmesan cheese
cooked spaghetti *or* noodles

Put Bel Paese, cream cheese and thin cream in top of double saucepan and cook slowly over hot water, stirring until smooth and creamy. Sauté the chopped mushrooms in butter for 5 minutes and add to sauce with chopped chicken, mixing well. Cook just until chicken is heated through, serve over cooked spaghetti or noodles and sprinkle with Parmesan cheese.

Chicken Puffs

Serve these for supper with Brown Mushroom Sauce (see page 145) or for a buffet party with mayonnaise.

3 cups cooked chicken, chopped fine	2 eggs, separated
1 tbsp butter *or* margarine	oil for deep frying
2 slices white bread	1 medium onion, finely chopped
2 tbsp hot water	salt and pepper

Sauté the onion in the butter for 10 minutes without browning, stirring frequently with a fork. Soak the bread, after cutting off crusts, in the hot water, then mash until smooth. Mix the cooked onion, chicken and bread mixture, season to taste and beat in egg yolks. Beat egg whites until stiff and fold into chicken mixture. Heat oil and drop spoonfuls of the mixture into hot oil, frying until golden and puffed up. Drain well on kitchen paper and serve at once.

A mixture of chicken and ham could be used for these puffs if there is not enough chicken. Put the meat through the fine blade of the mincer if a smoother mixture is preferred.

Chicken and Rice Pie

This is a change from the usual chicken pie.

1½ cups cooked chicken meat	½ cup diced celery
½ cup long grain rice	8 oz (200 g) puff pastry
3 hard-boiled eggs	1 tbsp chopped parsley
chicken stock	

Cook the rice in chicken stock until tender and drain well, retaining the stock. Place rice in bottom of a greased pie dish, cover with chicken pieces, parsley, celery and lastly the sliced eggs, first placing a pie funnel in the middle of the pie. Fill pie dish to within 1-inch (25 cm) from the top with cooled chicken stock, which may be made with a stock cube if necessary. Roll out pastry and place a strip round edge of dish, brush over with water and place pastry over the top, pressing edges firmly together. Cut a couple of gashes in pastry, decorate with pastry leaves and bake in hot oven (425°F, 220°C or No. 7) for 30 minutes, until golden and cooked through.

Lightly fried sliced mushrooms or sliced red or green peppers could be added to the pie for extra flavour.

Spiced Apples with Chicken
An unusual and very tasty dish from the Levant.

4 large cooking apples	pinch ground cinnamon
1 cup cooked, chopped chicken	pinch ground cloves
lemon juice	pinch ground ginger
½ cup soft breadcrumbs	pinch saffron
½ cup seedless raisins	brown sugar
¼ cup chopped walnuts	salt and pepper
butter	cooked rice

Wash apples and remove cores, but without taking the hole right through so the stuffing does not come out at the bottom. Place apples in boiling water with a little lemon juice and simmer for 5 minutes, then remove and drain well. Scoop out some of the centres to make more room for the stuffing. Soak raisins in hot water for 5 minutes, then drain.

Mix breadcrumbs with 2 tbsp melted butter, then add chicken, nuts, raisins, spices, salt and pepper and mix well together. Stuff apples with this mixture and place in a greased casserole or baking dish just big enough that the apples will stand firmly upright. Sprinkle each with a little brown sugar and dot with butter, add about 1-inch (25 cm) boiling water in the baking dish and bake in a moderate oven (350°F, 180°C or No. 4) for about 30 minutes. Be careful apples do not break while baking, cover with buttered paper if necessary. Serve each apple on a bed of cooked rice.

Hungarian Chicken
Quickly cooked and good over cooked rice or noodles.

2 good-size onions, chopped	¼ pint (150 ml) chicken stock
1 oz (25 g) butter *or* margarine	(may be made with stock-cube)
1 tbsp paprika	
1 tsp vinegar	8 oz (200 g) cooked chicken
2 tsp flour	5 fl oz (150 ml) carton sour cream
salt and pepper	

Fry onions lightly in butter, stir in paprika and cook for 4 or

5 minutes, stirring continuously. Stir in vinegar, seasoning and flour, then gradually stir in stock, stirring for about 3 minutes. Cut cooked chicken into small pieces and add to pan with sour cream, cook gently until heated through, but do not allow to boil. Serve over cooked rice or noodles.

Chicken and Mushroom Pasties

Good to take on a picnic, or for school lunches.

8 oz (200 g) puff pastry
2 tbsp butter *or* margarine
6–8 small mushrooms
1½ cups diced, cooked chicken
1½ tbsp flour

1 cup chicken stock
2 tbsp cream or top of the milk
pinch mixed herbs
salt and pepper

Roll out pastry and cut into 4-inch (10 cm) squares. Heat butter in saucepan and fry the chopped mushrooms for a few minutes. Stir in flour, then stir in the stock and cook until thickened, stirring all the time. Simmer for 5 minutes, then add chicken and herbs. Remove from heat, add cream and season. Cool slightly, then put a couple of spoonfuls of the mixture on half of each pastry square, fold other half over and pinch edges firmly together. Place on greased baking sheet and bake in a fairly hot oven (400°F, 200°C, No. 6) until golden and well risen.

Budin de Pain

This is really a chicken and bread pudding, and I have only tasted it in Belgium, a country where you find excellent beer which many Belgian housewives use in cooking various dishes. This is a very tasty way of using leftovers to make an unusual dish.

3 cups minced chicken
6 slices toast, buttered
½ cup chicken stock
½ cup beer
½ cup grated Parmesan cheese

2 tbsp melted butter
freshly ground black pepper
1 tbsp chopped parsley
½ cup soft breadcrumbs

Cut crusts from toast, and arrange toast in one layer in a buttered baking dish. Mix stock and beer together and pour over the toast, leave for ten minutes.

Mix the minced (or finely chopped) chicken with half the

cheese, melted butter, pepper and parsley, mixing well together. Spread this mixture evenly over the toast, mix breadcrumbs and remainder of cheese together and sprinkle over the top. Bake in a moderately hot oven (375°F, 190°C or No. 5) for about 45 minutes.

Delaware Chicken Shortcake

I tasted this delicious way of using chicken on a visit to Delaware, where it was served over corn bread squares, but I prefer it with freshly made scone rounds, allowing one 4-inch (10 cm) scone for each serve. Add a dash of pepper and some finely chopped parsley to the scone mixture.

For the filling:

2 tbsp butter *or* margarine
2 tbsp flour
2½ cups chicken stock
salt and pepper to taste

¼ lb (100 g) mushrooms
1 tbsp butter (extra)
3 cups diced, cooked chicken
scone rounds

While scones are baking make up the filling. Melt 2 tbsp butter or margarine in a pan, stir in flour and cook for 1 minute, then stir in stock and cook over low heat, stirring until smooth and thickened. Melt the extra butter in another pan, sauté the sliced mushrooms for several minutes, then add chicken pieces and gradually stir in sauce, heating all together just to boiling point. Season to taste.

Split scones open and butter if desired, place bottom halves on plates and cover with chicken mixture, cover with top halves and cover with more chicken. Garnish each with a sprig of parsley and serve at once.

In New England, where oysters are plentiful, they are sometimes used instead of mushrooms with the chicken.

Croquettes Milanese

Chicken pieces are combined with either cooked ham or tongue for this recipe.

1 cup finely chopped chicken
1 cup finely chopped ham *or* tongue
½ cup chopped red *or* green peppers
½ cup cooked macaroni

2 tbsp grated Parmesan cheese
thick white sauce
2 beaten eggs
1 tsp olive oil
fine, browned breadcrumbs
oil *or* fat for deep frying

Mix chicken, ham or tongue, macaroni, peppers, cheese and just enough white sauce to bind mixture together. Shape mixture into croquettes and put aside to chill for several hours. When ready to cook, beat eggs and oil together and dip croquettes into this, then into crumbs, making sure they are well coated on all sides. Deep fry in hot oil or fat until golden brown, then drain well on kitchen paper and serve at once.

Chicken in the Ring

This makes a little chicken go a long way. It is baked in a ring-mould, similar to that used for cakes with a hole in the middle.

For the ring:

½ lb (200 g) noodles *or* macaroni
2 eggs, beaten
½ cup soft white breadcrumbs
½ pint (250 ml) milk
1 cup grated cheese
1 tsp Worcestershire sauce
salt and pepper to taste

For the filling:

1 tbsp butter *or* margarine
2 tbsp flour
¾ pint (400 ml) milk
salt and pepper to taste
2 cups diced, cooked chicken
2 tbsp cooked, chopped ham
1 tsp grated onion
½ sweet red pepper, chopped
1 tbsp chopped parsley
½ lb (200 g) green peas

Drop noodles or macaroni into fast boiling, salted water and boil until tender, about 8 minutes. Drain well, add eggs, milk, cheese, breadcrumbs and seasonings. Turn into greased ring-mould, stand ring in a baking dish of water and bake in moderate oven (350°F, 180°C or No. 4) until set, about 45 minutes.

While ring is baking make the filling. Melt butter or margarine in a thick pan, stir in flour and cook for 1 minute. Slowly stir in milk, stirring until sauce thickens and boils. Add onion, parsley, chicken, ham and red pepper (be sure to remove the seeds) and cook for a few minutes, stirring occasionally.

When noodle ring is cooked, unmould on to a hot serving plate and fill middle with hot chicken mixture. Arrange cooked peas around the ring and serve at once.

Chicken Pancakes

The same filling as used for the noodle ring makes a good filling for pancakes which are an ideal supper dish.

Make up the pancakes from your favourite recipes, allowing two per person. Place a good spoonful of the filling mixture on each pancake and roll up, placing the filled pancakes in a buttered ovenproof baking dish, side by side. Pour any extra chicken mixture over the top of the pancakes, or sprinkle with grated cheese, cover with a lid or foil and reheat in the oven for about 20 minutes.

Curried Chicken in Grapefruit

These look as good as they taste as a starter for a dinner party for four, or serve them for lunch, cooked in individual ovenproof ramekins if possible.

2 large grapefruit
1½ cups cooked, diced chicken
1 tbsp butter *or* margarine
1 tbsp flour
1 cup chicken stock
2 tsp curry powder (*or* to taste)

1 tsp grated onion
2 tsp chopped parsley
2 tbsp peeled, chopped apple
soft white breadcrumbs
1 tbsp melted butter
salt and pepper

Cut each grapefruit in halves and remove pulp, cutting it into pieces, but be careful to remove any white pith and membranes. Put half the pulp aside—this can be served for breakfast.

Melt butter in a thick pan, stir in flour and curry powder and cook for 2 minutes, then stir in chicken stock, stirring until smooth and thickened. Add onion, apple, salt and pepper and simmer for 5 minutes, then add chicken, half the well-drained grapefruit pieces, and parsley. Divide this mixture between the four grapefruit cases, which should be placed in individual ovenproof dishes or in a casserole large enough to hold the four filled grapefruit halves firmly upright. Toss the breadcrumbs in the melted butter over low heat until just lightly golden, then sprinkle over the chicken mixture. Bake in moderate oven (350°F, 180°C or No. 4) for 15 to 20 minutes, until top is golden brown and mixture hot. Serve at once.

Chicken Crispies

Serve these as a hot snack, or with pre-dinner drinks.

½ lb (200 g) cold mashed potatoes

1 small egg, beaten
2–3 tbsp crushed cornflakes

4 to 5 oz (100–125 g) chopped chicken   fat *or* oil for frying

Mix chicken and potatoes together and form into small balls with floured hands. Dip in beaten egg, then in cornflakes until well coated all over. Fry in hot fat or oil until golden brown and crisp. If any stuffing is left over from the chicken, a little can be added to the chicken and potato mixture.

Chicken with Asparagus

1 small can asparagus spears
1 pint (500 ml) chicken stock
3 oz (75 g) butter
3 oz (75 g) flour
¼ pint (150 ml) single cream
2 tsp lemon juice
salt and pepper
2 hard-boiled eggs
about 1 lb (400 g) chicken meat, diced

Drain liquor from asparagus and make up to 1¼ pint (650 ml) with chicken stock (may be made with a cube). Melt butter in a pan, stir in flour and cook for 1 minute, then stir in stock and asparagus juice and keep stirring until boiling. Stir in cream and then the lemon juice, season to taste and simmer gently for several minutes, stirring occasionally.

Slice the eggs. Put aside 4 or 5 heads of asparagus and chop remainder. Add chicken, asparagus and one egg to the sauce and heat without boiling, then turn into a heated serving dish. Garnish with asparagus heads and slices of egg.

Spanish Chicken and Rice

1 cup long grain rice
2½ cups chicken stock
4 to 6 oz (100 to 150 g) chicken meat, diced
2 rashers lean bacon, chopped
1 medium onion, chopped
6 mushrooms, sliced
2 tbsp tomato paste
2 tsp Worcestershire sauce

Bring stock to the boil, if necessary use chicken cubes, add rice and cook for 10 minutes, stirring once. Add remainder of ingredients, stirring well, then cook very slowly, uncovered, until liquid has evaporated, about 35 to 40 minutes. Stir at intervals to prevent rice catching on the pan.

Chicken and Corn Pie

8 oz (200 g) short pastry
8 to 10 oz (200 to 250 g) chicken, cooked and diced
1 small can creamed sweetcorn
1 tbsp chopped parsley
1 tbsp chopped red pepper *or* 3 or 4 sliced mushrooms
salt and pepper

Roll out pastry to fit over a round pie-dish. Mix remainder of ingredients together and put into pie-dish, cover with pastry and bake in a hot oven (425°F, 220°C or No. 7) until pastry is cooked and golden brown. A little chicken stock or top of the milk may be added if necessary to keep mixture moist.

Chicken for Slimmers

For those who want to lose weight or just keep to the weight they are, chicken is an ideal food. Low-calorie protein foods served as the basis of your dieting meals are a sure way to speed your weight loss and chicken, lower in calories than nearly all other meats and one of the lowest calorie protein foods of all, makes an ideal choice – and is also economical.

Chicken has hardly any fat, which is what makes chicken so low in calories. By comparing the figures below for roast meats you can see why it is such a good choice for slimmers.

Roast chicken	47 calories per oz (25 g)
„ sirloin beef	109 „ „ „
„ topside beef	91 „ „ „
„ leg of lamb	83 „ „ „
„ leg of pork	90 „ „ „
„ turkey	56 „ „ „
„ veal	66 „ „ „

Even if only one member of the family is really serious about dieting, the main dishes given here will be quite acceptable to all, which means that it is not necessary to cook special dishes just for one. In the case of roast chicken the dieter would be wise not to eat the stuffing or the bread sauce and gravy which usually accompanies it, but the basic roast can be enjoyed without such trimmings.

Chicken and Vegetable Soup

1½ pints (850 ml) chicken stock
½ oz (15 g) long grain rice
1 small onion, chopped
1 small carrot, chopped
½ stick celery, chopped

2 whole cloves
small blade of mace tied in muslin
salt and pepper to taste
2 tbsp chopped parsley

Be sure all fat is removed from stock. Put stock, vegetables, rice and muslin bag into saucepan and bring to the boil. Simmer for 15–20 minutes until rice is soft and vegetables cooked. Remove muslin bag, adjust seasoning, add parsley, serve. Serves 4; 25 calories per serve.

Watercress Soup

1 small onion, finely chopped
2 tsp butter
1 bunch watercress
1½ pints (850 ml) chicken stock
1 tsp dried skimmed milk powder
salt and pepper

Wash watercress well and chop small. Melt butter in pan and lightly fry chopped onion, add watercress and stir in stock. Simmer for 10 minutes, add milk powder, season to taste and serve. Serves 4; 25 calories per serve.

Coq au Vin

This is a slimming version of a very famous French dish which is almost as tasty as the original (see p. 50).

4 oz (100 g) button mushrooms
12 button onions, *or* 1 large onion, sliced
½ oz (15 g) butter
1 tbsp oil
4 chicken quarters (8 oz or 200 g each)
8 fl oz (200 ml) red wine
½ pint (250 ml) chicken stock made with 1 stock cube
bouquet garni
pinch ground nutmeg
salt and pepper to taste
2 tbsp plain flour

Wash or peel mushrooms, peel onions and fry in the mixture of butter and oil for 5 minutes, until onions are lightly browned. Remove from pan and place in ovenproof casserole. Fry chicken quarters in the same pan for 5 to 8 minutes, turning to brown on all sides. Remove and put into casserole with onions and mushrooms, add bouquet garni. Stir flour into fat remaining in pan and cook for 2 minutes, then stir in the wine and stock, bring to boil and continue stirring until the mixture thickens. Add nutmeg and season to taste, then pour sauce over chicken. Cover casserole and cook in a moderate oven (350°F, 180°C or No. 4) for 45 to 60 minutes, until the chicken is tender when tested. Remove bouquet garni before serving. Serves 4; 380 calories per serve.

Country Chicken Casserole

8 chicken drumsticks
2 tbsp plain flour
2¼ oz (63 g) can tomato purée
1 pint (500 ml) chicken stock

salt and pepper
½ tsp mixed herbs
1 tbsp oil
½ oz (15 g) butter
2 small onions, sliced
4 small carrots, sliced

made from 1 chicken stock cube
1 bay leaf
4 oz (100 g) frozen peas
1 tbsp parsley, chopped

Put flour, salt and pepper and mixed herbs into a large brown paper bag and put the drumsticks, two at a time, into the bag, shaking well until chicken is coated all over. Repeat until all legs are well coated with the flour. Heat oil and butter in a frying pan large enough to take the chicken legs in one layer. Fry drumsticks for 5 minutes until golden brown on all sides. Transfer them to an ovenproof casserole. Mix tomato purée into chicken stock and pour over the casserole, add bay leaf and a little additional seasoning, but remember the stock is well seasoned. Cover and cook in a moderate oven (350°F, 180°C or No. 4) for about ¾ hour or until chicken is tender. Add the peas half-way through cooking time. Remove bay leaf and sprinkle parsley over the top before serving. Serves 4; 340 calories per serve.

Chicken Pie

8 oz (200 g) cooked chicken
4 oz (100 g) sliced, cooked carrots
4 oz (100 g) cooked cauliflower sprigs
1 tbsp chopped parsley

1 bay leaf
1 tbsp cornflour
½ pint (250 ml) chicken stock made from ½ stock cube
½ lb (200 g) frozen puff pastry
milk to glaze

Put chicken, carrots, cauliflower, parsley and bay leaf into an 8 in. (20 cm) pie dish. Blend cornflour with a little cold stock, heat remainder of stock and stir in blended cornflour, stirring until boiling and thickened, season to taste and pour over chicken and vegetables in casserole.

Thaw pastry and roll out to fit pie dish, sealing the edges firmly. Brush top over with milk and bake in a hot oven (450°F, 230°C or No. 8) for 25 to 30 minutes until pastry is golden brown and cooked through. Serves 4; 350 calories per serve.

Chicken Pilaff

10 oz (250 g) cooked chicken,
   in thick slices
1 orange
1 lemon
¾ (400 ml) pint chicken stock

salt and pepper to taste
5 oz (125 g) long grain rice
1 oz (25 g) butter
1 oz (25 g) seedless raisins
   plumped in boiling water

Grate peel from the orange and lemon. Squeeze lemon and add juice to chicken stock. Season to taste. Simmer rice in the stock until tender, about 15 minutes. Add butter, raisins and shredded orange and lemon rind to rice, mix well.

Place half rice mixture in an ovenproof serving dish, add a layer of chicken slices, then cover with remaining rice. Re-heat in a warm oven before serving. Serves 4; 350 calories per serve.

Chicken with Green Pepper

4 chicken quarters
   (8 oz or 200 g each)
½ oz (15 g) butter, melted
salt and pepper
1 onion, chopped
1 oz (25 g) butter *or* margarine

1 oz (25 g) plain flour
½ pint (250 ml) stock made
   from ½ chicken stock cube
1 green pepper
1 carton natural yogurt

Brush chicken quarters with melted butter, season with salt and pepper and put under moderate grill, skin side down, and grill for 15–20 minutes, turning half-way through cooking time.

Meanwhile, melt butter in saucepan and fry onion gently for 5 minutes without browning. Stir in flour and cook for 2 minutes, stir in stock and bring to boil, stirring, then simmer for 2 minutes. Remove stalk, pith and seeds from green pepper and cut into strips, cover with boiling water for 3 minutes, then drain, add to sauce and simmer gently for 5 minutes, stirring at intervals. When chicken is cooked, place on a heated serving dish, stir yogurt into sauce and warm gently, then pour just enough over the chicken to coat pieces. Serve rest separately. Serves 4; 380 calories per serve.

Chicken and Mushroom Fricassee

2½ lb (1·2 kg) chicken
1 large onion, chopped
1 large carrot, sliced
4 oz (100 g) mushrooms, sliced
¾ pint (400 ml) water
¼ pint (150 ml) skimmed milk
bouquet garni
salt and pepper
1 oz (25g) butter
1 oz (25 g) plain flour
1 tbsp chopped parsley
4 lemon wedges

Cut chicken into 8 sections and put into large saucepan with vegetables, water, skimmed milk, bouquet garni, salt and pepper. Bring slowly to the boil, cover and simmer gently for 1 hour or until chicken is tender. Remove from heat, strain off liquor and reserve.

Melt butter in a clean saucepan, add flour and cook 2 minutes, gradually stir in chicken liquor, continue stirring until it boils and thickens. Add chicken and vegetables, simmer for 2 minutes. Serve garnished with parsley and lemon wedges. Serves 4; 400 calories per serve.

Chicken and Orange Salad

3 juicy oranges
12 oz (300 g) cooked chicken
2 bunches watercress
2 tbsp wine vinegar
2 sweetener tablets, crushed
salt and pepper

Peel 2 of the oranges, carefully removing all the white pith. Slice oranges and mix with chicken pieces and watercress in a salad bowl. Squeeze juice from remaining orange and mix with vinegar, sweetener, salt and pepper, pour over salad and chill for half an hour before serving.

Be sure to collect the juice from the oranges which have been sliced to add to dressing. Serves 4; 215 calories per serve.

Acknowledgements

There is no such thing as an original recipe today—all are variations of basic themes, but I would like to thank all those people in many different countries who have shared their special recipes with me and allowed me to use them in this book, although sometimes in a slightly altered form to fit in with local ingredients.

I would also thank Mrs Gina Field and her staff at the British Poultry Information Service, and Buxted Poultry Ltd for their assistance.

Index

Agda's Fried 68
  and Almond Casserole 63
Almond Chicken Legs 79
American Cooking Terms 5
Andorran Paella 86
  with Apples, Spiced 164
  with Artichoke Hearts 65
  and Asparagus Mould 111
  with Asparagus 169
  Austrian with Noodles 52
  Avocado Suprêmes 103

Bahamas Casserole 90
Baked with Pineapple 61
Boiled 29
Brandied with Peaches 42
Breasts or Suprêmes 135
    Chianti 139
    in foil 141
    Garibaldi 140
    au Gratin 136
    and Ham Rolls 142
    with Hazelnuts 141
    Kiev 137
    with Lemon Sauce 135
    a la Marsala 140
    Missouri 138
    Piquant 139
    St Clair 136
    Soave 138
Brewer's 87
Budin de Pain 165
Butter Baste 159

California Bake 80
California Marinade 159
Capon a la Basque 44
Captain's 91

and Carrot Mousse 109
and Celery Mould 108
Cheesey in a Basket 78
Cheshire 40
Chinese Glazed 49
Chop Suey 64
in Cider 58
Cock-a-Leekie 39
in Cognac 89
Cold Lemon 107
Coolangatta 70
Coq au Riesling 50
Coq au Vin 50, 173
and Corn Pie 170
and Corn Salad 110
Country Casserole 173
Country-Style, Grilled 71
Crètan 41
Crispies 168
Croquettes Milanese 166
Curried in Grapefruit 168
Curried with Spaghetti 38
Curry Honolulu 66
Cypriot, Rice Stuffed 34

Delaware Shortcake 166
Devilled in Denmark 88
Devil's Grilled 96
Devonshire 59
Double Crust Pie 75
Drumsticks, Honeyed 61
Drumsticks in Pastry 76
Drunken 115
Dutch Casserole 82

Enchiladas with Chili Sauce 69

Facts about Chicken 9

Flaming with Cherries 97
Florida Salad 107
Freezing 10
French Cooking Terms 11
Fried Viennese 82

Giblets 12
Glazed, Cold 114
Greek Lemon 87
Greek Pilaff 162
with Green Pepper 175
Grosvenor House Pie 73
Gruyère Surprise Packet 70

and Ham Pie, Cold 116
and Ham Potpie 56
and Ham Rolls with
 Pineapple 111
Herb Marinade 159
Herbed with Olives 83
Herbs for Flavour 14
Herby Pie 96
Hollywood 79
Honeyed Drumsticks 61
Honeyed Legs 77
Honeyed Legs, Grilled 77
Honeyed with Peaches 48
Hungarian 164
Hungarian Smitane 31

Introduction 2
Irish 84

Javanese Marinade 159

Kansas City 51
Kebabs 158
Kebab, Whole Chicken 159
Kentish Pie 56
Kentish Pudding 84
Kiev 137
King of Prussia's

Favourite Dish 131
Kitchen Equipment 6

and Leek Pie 37
Lemon 40
Lemon-Garlic Parcels 95
Lemon Marinade 158
Livers 124
 Appetizers 133
 Budapest 131
 Chinese Style 128
 Curried 132
 Deep Fried 126
 Espagnole 130
 Florentine 127
 Jerez 124
 Pancakes 129
 Piquant 125
 Risotto 126
 Spiced 129
 Spread 119
 Sweet-Sour 128
 Tartlets 133
 with Tomatoes 125
 Tyrolean 132
 Veneziana 132
 Vol-au-Vents 127
Louisiana 93

and Macaroni Pudding 92
Madeira 59
Malayan Spiced 60
Marengo 89
Marinaded Grilled 71
Marinades
 California 159
 Herb 150, 159
 Honey-orange 150
 Javanese 159
 Lemon 158
 Pineapple 159
 Wine 150, 159

180

Market Day 45
Maryland 94
Meal in a Pot 72
Mediterranean 53
Melon Luncheon Salad 112
Mexicana 33
Minted Grill 98
Mousse 115
Mozzarella 99
and Mushroom Fricassee 176
and Mushroom Pasties 165
and Mushroom Salad 108
Mustard in Foil 51

Nasturtium Salad 103
Navaressa 55
New England Boiled Dinner 45
Normandy 41
North of England Pie 75
and Onion Bake 31
Orange Glazed 32
and Orange Salad 176
and Oyster Pie 74

Pacific Coconut Bake 66
Paella 98
Pancake 167
Paprika 80
Parmesan au Gratin 68
Patés and Spreads
  Curry Spread 120
  Ham & Chicken Paté 117
  Liver & Cheese Spread 119
  Liver Paté with Black
    Olives 121
  Liver Spread 119
  Liver Terrine 119
  Mixed Liver Paté 117
  Potted Spread 116
  Rosemary Paté 118
  Terrine 120
Pie for Slimmers 174

Pie Pretoria 74
Pilaff for Slimmers 175
Pilaff St Hubert 85
Pineapple Marinade 159
Piquant Danish Salad 101
Plate Pie 76
Pollo Espagnole 81
Potato Ring 101
Portuguese Pink 36
Poule en Daube 43
Poule au Pot 42
Poulet aux Crevettes 65
Poussin Arabian 35
and Prawn Pilaff 93
Pretoria Pie 74
Provençal Casserole 63
Puffs 163

with Rice 54
Rice Medley 106
and Rice Pie 163
and Rice Ring 106
and Rice Ring Salad 106
in the Ring 167
Roast 29
Roast with Pineapple 32
Russian Pirog 73
Russian with Raisins 55
Russian Spring 94

Salads 101
Salad Caprice 112
Salad Caracas 109
Salad Geneva 102
Salad Niçoise 105
with Salsa Verde 113
Sauces 144
  Bechamel 144
  Blended Curry 146
  Bread 144
  Brown Mushroom 145
  Coating Mayonnaise 149

Sauces—*cont.*
  Cold Curry 150
  French Dressing 147
  Hollandaise, Quick 146
  Indonesian 147
  Mayonnaise 148
  Mayonnaise Variations 149
  Mayonnaise Verte 148
  Mixed Herb 145
  Paprika 145
  Piquant 147
  Tomato 146
Sesame 87
Skewered Poussins 160
for Slimmers 172
Somerset 30
Soubise 49
Soups 17
  Bacon & Corn Chowder 22
  Basic Stock 17
  and Cheese 27
  Consommé Avocado 20
  in the Corn Chowder 27
  Cream of Celery 21
  Creamy 17
  Creme St Germain 19
  Creole 24
  Egg Drop 21
  Egg & Lemon 21
  German Giblet 18
  Giblet, Pressure Cooked 18
  Hurry-Curry 26
  Liver & Noodle 25
  Majorcan 23
  Minestra di Fagioli 25
  Petite Marmite 19
  Potage Crecy 23
  Potage du Barry 26
  Potage Paysanne 22
  Pumpkin 26
  Rice with Livers 20
  Russian Rice & Lemon 25

  Summer Day Avocado 20
  and Vegetable 18
  and Vegetable for
  Slimmers 172
  Watercress for Slimmers 173
  Zuppa Pavese 24
Spaghetti Florentine 127
Spanish Ragout 95
Spanish with Rice 169
Spiced with Mushrooms 92
Spiced Pot Roast 47
Spit-Roasted 30
Steamed 29
Stuffings 151
  Anchovy & Lemon 153
  Bacon & Parsnip 154
  Carrot & Orange 155
  Ham & Olives 151
  Ham & Rice 153
  Liver & Mushroom 152
  Mushroom & Onion 153
  Nutty-Herb with Wine 153
  Orange & Herbs 152
  Parsley & Celery 154
  Rice & Raisin 151
  Sausage & Garlic 152
Stuffed Tomatoes 102
Summer Curry Salad 107
Surfer's Paradise Salad 110
Sussex Crispy 81
Swedish Cold Curried 113
Sweet-Sour 79

Tandoori 35
with Tarragon 46
Terrine 120
Texan in a Basket 78
Tonnato 104
Trinidad 83

Verona 162
Viennese Fried 82

Viennese Style 60
Vieux Carré 52
Virginia Pie 48

Waldorf Salad 108
Walnut Loaf 62

Waterzoie 54
Weights, Measures and
    Temperatures
Welsh 37
in White Wine 72
Wine Marinade 159

NOTES

NOTES

NOTES